THE DIVINE LIFE IN MAN

AND OTHER SERMONS

The Divine Life in Man

And other Sermons

BY

FREDERICK A. NOBLE, D.D., LL.D.

Author of "Typical New Testament Conversions,"
"Discourses on Philippians," "Our Redemption."

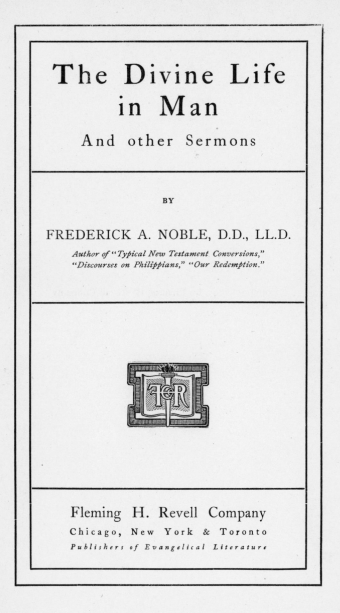

Fleming H. Revell Company

Chicago, New York & Toronto

Publishers of Evangelical Literature

TO THE MEMORY OF ONE

LOVING AND BELOVED

WHO FOR FOUR AND THIRTY YEARS MADE MY
HOME SWEET WITH HER GRACIOUS PRESENCE
AND WHO SHARED WITH ME THE BURDENS
AND JOYS OF THE CHRISTIAN MINISTRY

LUCY PERRY NOBLE

THIS VOLUME

IS TENDERLY AND REVERENTLY DEDICATED

"Upon thy brow
A wreath whose flowers no earthly soil have known,
Woven of the beatitudes."

CONTENTS.

———

5

THE DIVINE LIFE IN MAN.

And God created man in His own image. Gen. 1: 27.

That through these ye may become partakers of the divine nature. 2 Peter 1: 4.

Our Father which art in heaven. Matt. 6: 9.

The Spirit himself beareth witness with our spirit, that we are children of God. Rom. 8: 16.

I am .....the Life. John 14: 6.

I came that they may have life, and may have it abundantly. John 10: 10.

Till we all attain unto....the measure of the stature of the fullness of Christ. Eph. 4: 13.

ON the basis and warrant of these very remarkable scriptures it is my purpose to say something this morning concerning *The Divine Life in Man.*

The conception of the possibility of a divine life in man is the highest tribute which can be paid to the dignity of human nature. According to this conception man is great, not merely because he is rational, endowed with the faculties of reason and conscience, but because his rationality has living connection and kinship with the Supreme Rationality of the universe. This conception, too, which holds in it such tribute to the dignity of human nature, and which implies so many other qualities of the highest significance, is a fact which was realized in the original creation of man, and which is realized anew as

7

often as any soul comes under the regenerating power of the gospel and is born into the kingdom.

This is what is brought out with an almost startling distinctness in the group of passages standing at the head of this discourse. Man, like God, is personal and spiritual. He has the source of his being in God. He has come into life in virtue of the breath of God in his soul. He has a certain intellectual and moral likeness to God; and by cultivation and discipline this likeness may be advanced till his thought and will reflect, in some measure, the thought and will of God, and all his movements and desires are in the direction of God. He may yield his whole nature—all his powers and faculties—up to the guidance of God, and the current of an exalted fellowship may flow back and forth between his heart and the heart of God. Having fallen out of this fellowship, and lost this divine life, through sin, he may yet find it again through faith in the Son of God, who came into the world for the express purpose of renewing men dead in trespasses and sins, and restoring the marred image in which they were made. He may have inward witness that God is his Father, and that he is God's child. He may know and enjoy God.

These are general statements covering the case. The further development of the subject will be promoted best by asking two or three questions.

I. *What is the standard and type of this divine life in man?*

Or to put the same question in another form, were one to realize this divine life in anything like completeness what manner of man would he be? The answer is at hand and has already been given in the passage in which the great Apostle identifies loftiest aspirations and highest attainments with the measure of the fullness of the stature of Christ. He would be a man after the pattern of Christ. He would be pure like Christ, but like Christ he would be grieved and indignant at the sight of wrong. He would be wise and pertinent in all his actions to times and seasons and duties like Christ. He would be loving and gentle like Christ. He would be open to all heavenly communications and heavenly fellowships like Christ. He would be in sympathy with the sorrows and woes of humanity like Christ. He would be vicarious in the temper of his mind, and would rejoice in nothing so much as in putting his shoulder under the burdens of the over-burdened, and in being in every way helpful like Christ. Like Christ he would walk with God, and we should see once more—what was seen by all eyes which had any spiritual vision in them when the Divine Man was walking the ways of this dusty earth in Palestine—a man pressing his steps on through life with one hand locked in the hand of the Father and the other locked in the hand of such of his fellow-creatures as might be in special need of guidance and strength. He would be a man at once so sweet and lofty, so human and so heavenly, that his life would go far toward interpreting to us the profound meaning of the incarnation.

But in getting up into this attainment of the measure of the stature of the fullness of Christ, or—what is the same thing—the realization of a life which moves forward on the line of the life of Christ, and of a character which is built up on the model of the character of Christ, we get up also into the attainment and realization of all the other promises and possibilities set before us in the passages under review.

The image of God in which man was made is brought out and restored. For what is this image and what does the possession of it imply? Personality of being,—not absorption in the mass of things, but personality, spirituality, or a soul to master matter and use it for noble ends; mind to see and apprehend truth; moral sense to distinguish between right and wrong; spontaneous approval of holiness; and capacity to make known our thoughts and desires to God, and to receive from God knowledge and strength and joy. But to enumerate these elements which enter into the original likeness of man to God is simply to describe Jesus Christ in the perfection of His humanity. To see Him is to see one in whom this likeness is brought out with an absolute accuracy. To be a man after the type of Jesus Christ is to be a man after the primary and ideal conception of man.

By the same process, and to the same extent, we become partakers of the divine nature. These are marvelous words which have just been on our lips,—

made in the image of God. So, too, are the
words of Peter marvelous when he speaks of our
becoming partakers of the divine nature: "Whereby
He hath granted unto us His precious and exceeding
great promises; that through these ye may become
partakers of the divine nature, having escaped from
the corruption that is in the world by lust." There
is a possible union of the soul with God in love and
view and aim so close, that what God is may be
known, in part at least, from what is seen and felt of
Him in the soul. It was on the basis of this sublime
possibility that our Lord offered the prayer: "That
they may all be one; even as thou, Father, art in me,
and I in thee, *that they also may be in us.*" This is
to come into such full and joyous identification with
God in all the outgoings of His life that the pulse of
thought and purpose which beats in Him has response in the pulse of thought and purpose which
beats in the soul. It is to think with God; it is to
feel with God; it is to will with God. It is to love
what God loves and hate what God hates, and throw
all one's energies on the side of His righteousness.
Once more, however, just simply to state what it is
to be a partaker of the divine nature is to set forth
Christ. To look on Christ is to behold a living illustration of this high achievement. To be like Christ
is to share with Him in His partakership in the divine nature.

We come also into a sense of sonship. Christ has
put into our mouths the great words: "Our Father."

There is no higher height of distinction to which we can climb. For if God be our Father, then are we God's children. His blood is in our veins. His characteristics mark us. His greatness and goodness and love and majesty and power and purity become to us the ground of a peculiar joy. His glory will He not give to another, but His children are born into a portion in it. To be able to say "Our Father" in the faith and sincerity and love in which Jesus wishes us to say the words is to take our place in the family immortal and blessed, whose head is God, the Divine Father, and whose Elder Brother is the Son of God, and whose glad members are made up, in part, of those who have kept their first estate, and, in part, of those who have been redeemed by the blood of the Lamb slain from the foundation of the world. This, again, is all secured in the attainment of the measure of the stature of the fullness of Christ. To reach this fullness is to awaken in the soul a deep and tender and abiding sense of sonship. It no longer seems a thing incongruous to speak of God as our Father, and of ourselves as His children; but we fall into the use of these terms, and into the relationship implied in them, as easily and naturally as sons and daughters who have been born into sweet earthly homes fall into the use of them. God is our Creator still, and we are His creatures? Yes, but we are more,—we are children. God is our Sovereign still, and we are His subjects and owe Him obedience? Yes; but we are more,—we are children. This is what He himself in His Word delights to tell us. "Ye received the Spirit of adoption, whereby we cry: Abba, Father. The Spirit himself beareth witness with our spirit, that we are children of God; and if children, then heirs; heirs of God and joint heirs with Christ."

To reach, then, the measure of the stature of the fullness of Christ is to reach it all. It is to reach such likeness to God in thought and character as is implied in being made in the image of God. It is to reach the intimate and sacred fellowship with God naturally suggested when we speak of becoming a partaker of the divine nature. It is to reach the high place where we can stand up and exclaim in terms of exultation: "Now we are children of God." The standard and type of this divine life are found, embodied and exemplified, in Christ. If a man would know exactly what to struggle for in trying to realize to perfection the divine life, or if a man would know what the divine life, after being quickened in the soul, and unhindered in its development, will come to, he may see it all in Christ. To attain unto the measure of the stature of the fullness of Christ is to realize the divine life in the highest and completest form possible on earth.

II. *How is this divine life in man to be developed into its fairest and amplest proportions?*

The answers to this question are many and varied. There are some answers which would be given in common by all who have ever paid any attention to

the conditions and laws of spiritual growth. There
are still other answers which would be colored by
temperament, or circumstances, or peculiar experiences, and which would have value just in the ratio
in which they might fit into the temperaments, or circumstances, or peculiar experiences of those to whom
they should be given. There are further answers
which might create not a little suspicion when first
announced, but nevertheless might have in them
marked worth to large numbers of people.

The end in view, it must be borne in mind, is not
to get the divine life developed in part, or in some
single feature or element of it, but to get it built up
in its entireness—unfolded until it is complete in its
sweetness and symmetry and strength.

1. *First, then, as one of the ways in which this
divine life in man may be developed into its fairest
and amplest proportions, there may be mentioned a
profounder study of nature, and a quicker, heartier
sympathy with all the movements and disclosures of
nature.*

Nature is God's creation. All the laws and
methods of nature are emanations from the divine
mind. The Father of our spirits is the Maker of the
stars and the rocks and the lilies. God speaks to
us in all forms of life and beauty. Nature is not
agnostic. Nature is witness to the wisdom and power
of God. In every sound she utters, from the chirp
of a cricket on the hearth and the sighing of the
winds through the tree-tops, to the ceaseless roar of

Niagara and the awful reverberations of thunder in the Alps, Nature is eloquent in praise of God. God's sign-manual is on every page of the majestic volume of Nature.

It is an unutterable misfortune for Science and Religion to drift apart. If Science loses its bearings, and goes astray, without the guidance of Religion, so Religion eliminates one of the strong factors of its support, and is the weaker for it, when it refuses to make the most of the deductions of Science. Taking this course it has to walk half-crippled and timidly where it might walk erect and with a firm tread. We get an indispensable conception of God from the Sermon on the Mount. We also get an indispensable conception of God from the Mount on which the Sermon was delivered. If we are to be large and full in our divine life, and to stand in all-around accord with God in His activities, we cannot afford to forego the great and precious lessons God would teach us through the countless material facts and forms of the outer world.

It is true there have been scientists in the past, as there are scientists now, who claimed to be able to see no traces in Nature of a creative, designing and superintending mind. But this does not alter the fact. God is not shut out of the universe, and out of existence, because there are some men who refuse to see and acknowledge Him.

There are men who read the Bible, and yet can see no evidence of the presence of God in the book;

but this blindness does not set aside the inspiration of the Bible. There are men who have made a study of the human soul, — the mind with its wonderful powers, the conscience with its capacity for moral discriminations, who have yet come to the conclusion that these astonishing endowments count nothing in proof of the existence of God. All the same the mind in the very structure of it demands and demonstrates a God.

It is not otherwise with Nature. Nature does not cease to be God's voice, and the organ through which He speaks His thought, merely because there are some ears too gross and heavy to detect a divine accent in the utterance. There are atheistic botanists; but botany is not atheistic. There are atheistic geologists; but geology is not atheistic. There are atheistic astronomers; but astronomy is not atheistic. Every flower in the field, every bit of granite which lies packed away in the mountains, every star in the multitudinous constellations which shines down upon us out of the over-arching skies, every bird flitting from limb to limb and filling the air with strains of song, every flash of light, every manifestation of law, and every form of life from crawling worm to quiring angel, has in it a testimony to the wisdom and power and benignity of God. "The heavens declare the glory of God, and the firmament showeth His handiwork."

This leads to saying — what seems often to be overlooked — how large was the use of nature and how helpful, which was made by the Bible writers! Notably is this true of the Old Testament writers, and of our Lord as reproduced by the writers of the New Testament. To the Psalmist's eye heaven and earth alike were always a fresh display of the activities and splendors of God. The Prophets appear to have been as familiar with certain natural phenomena as are the most passionate novel readers with their favorite authors. In the thunder Job heard God. Lightning flashes and storm and heat and cold had for him most impressive lessons in divinity. May we forget who said "Behold the lilies"? There are wholesome theologies in lilies, in hills, in brooks, in meadows, in waving fields. Holy men of old appreciated the teachings of nature because they were so much alive to the presence of God in all the on-goings of nature. To leave out the lessons and influences of nature in our cultivation of the divine life within us is to leave out something which tends to give spiritual wholesomeness and breadth and solidity. Whether the facts are traced out and laid bare to us after the manner of Darwin and Dana and Newcomb and Wright, or whether the facts are interpreted and illuminated to our understanding by men of the genius of Ruskin and Bryant and Burr and Burroughs, there is nourishment in them for our spiritual faculties. To be blind to the presence of God in lakes and clouds and open skies and sweet broad landscapes and solemn forests and valleys and the sweep of mountains is to defraud our own souls. Robertson has told us that he read

the works of Jonathan Edwards, as he read the works
of other authors, till the ideas of Edwards became a
part of the iron atoms of his blood. He has also
told us that he was accustomed to go apart from men
and books, and wander out into the fields and groves
where he might feel God through what was about
him, and learn better to commune with Him and
adore His excellency. Jonathan Edwards likewise,
whom Robertson read to such profit, found God in the
fullness of an unutterable joy, not alone in the study
and closet, but out in the solitude of the field and
forest. In drawing his portrait of Martin Luther,
Carlyle seems to take special delight in putting in
those touches which reveal the great Reformer's clear
vision for the presence of God in nature, and showing
what sweet lessons he learned of God by simply lifting
his eyes and looking abroad on the world.

To have simple, harmonious and vigorous spiritual
life, open at all angles, and in sympathy with God
in all his movements and manifestations, one needs
more familiarity — very much more than the vast majority of us possess — with what God has written in
the great wide-open Book of Nature. It is healthy
and helpful. It is not possible for devout souls to
come near to nature without being enriched and
gladdened. The beloved Whittier, in a mood in
which he altogether underestimated his own genius,
lamented that he was obliged to look upon the "common forms" of Nature with "unanointed eyes;" but
it was he who sang in jubilant strains:

"The harp at Nature's advent strung
　　Has never ceased to play;
　The song the stars of morning sung
　　Has never died away.

　*　　　*　　　*　　　*　　　*

　So Nature keeps the reverent frame
　　With which her years began,
　And all her signs and voices shame
　　The prayerless heart of man."

2　*Another way in which the divine life within us may be developed into the fairest and amplest proportions is by tracing God and following along with God in the progressive unfolding of history.*

This world in which we live is not the devil's world. It does not belong to the devil. Men seem sometimes to be willing to turn it all over to his bad care, as though the right to it had somehow come to inhere in him; but it is not the devil's world, — it is God's world.

So history in the thought of some people appears to be only act after act in a long and appalling succession of violence and blood and treachery and deceit and the triumph of wrong. Color has been given to this view by the fact that not a few of the historians, like not a few of the scientists, have been men without any religious faith, and therefore men who have taken pains to leave the divine factor out of their accounts of the march of events. Motley could write the story of the awful struggle in the Netherlands, without giving any recognition to God and the part played by Providence in the conflict.

Buckle could write of civilization, just as though
civilization as we have come to know and enjoy it
was something apart from all divine agency. Hume
could chronicle the stages of development in the national life of England on the theory that what seemed
to be divine interposition from time to time in the interests of freedom and intelligence and the broadening rights of men were only fortuitous happenings.
Gibbon could bring his matchless skill and immense
learning into service in tracing "The Decline and Fall
of the Roman Empire," and tell the tale in a way
to ignore God, and to make the impression that the
causes of all this mighty growth and decay were
simply human.

But Motley and Buckle and Hume and Gibbon
alike failed in so far as they refused to admit God
into their several stories, for the reason that God was
in the woof and warp of the events they recorded and
could not be left out without harm to their narratives.
His name could be left out, and any positive recognition of His presence and service could be left out,
but God could not be left out. God was a living, in-
ruling and over-ruling Energy in all these historic
developments. He was not in Roman history in the
same way and for the same purpose that he was in
Israelitish history. He was not in English history
in the same way and for the same purpose, nor in
the history of Holland in the same way and for the
same purpose, that He was in Israelitish history.
Nevertheless He was in the history of each of these

peoples, — a potent, guiding and traceable Force. He has been present in all nations, and in all civilizations. His agency and intervention have been marked in our American history. He is at work in England and France and Germany, in Japan and China and Africa, and everywhere, to-day.

This is what is to be recognized if men would be intelligent and broad-minded in their faith. They must take wide views of God's working in the world, both as to the past and present, and cultivate the habit of seeing His movements in the rise and fall of empires, and in the progress of civilization, and in the victories of truth and righteousness. There is something tonic as well as broadening in this method of looking at events. It adds immensely to our confidence to feel that God is behind all the epoch-making men and the epoch-making measures; and that in the great transactions which have changed the face of society, and set humanity forward, He has been not a silent but an active agent.

To read the story of Columbus with God excluded from the record is to narrow thought and dwarf one's own manhood; but to read this story with God's presence recognized is to lend dignity to every human soul. It lifts us all to a higher plane, and makes life an interest of vaster moment. More than an epic grandeur attaches to the dauntless voyaging and state-building of the Pilgrim Fathers, because we are so sure all their movements were under the guidance of a divine wisdom. When we think of them as the chosen instruments of Providence for securing and maintaining liberty, Washington and Lincoln grow upon us, and we grow with them. To have no eye to see God in history and in current events is to be blind to some of the most impressive manifestations of God, and to deprive the soul of a source of knowledge and strength of which it stands often in special need.

3.   *Another way still in which the divine life within us may be developed into the fairest and amplest proportions is by recognizing God and learning what He has to teach as He has come into manifestation through literature.*

By this very much more is understood than the reading of books which are technically called books of devotion.   Even with this class of literature there is in general too little familiarity.   There would be less worldliness, less ignorance of the laws and conditions of spiritual life, and more faith in prayer, and more heart in worship, and more joy in all kinds of Christian service, were more time given by believers to such helps to growth in knowledge and grace as have been furnished in the devotional works of Thomas á Kempis and Bunyan and Baxter and Doddridge and Taylor and Howe and Tholuck and Rutherford and James and by the eminent writers of Sacred Poetry.

By this, too, very much more is understood than the reading of books which pertain exclusively to religious subjects.   It ought to go without saying that books on the existence and personality and attri-

butes of God; on the self-revelation and moral government of God; on the history of the church from the
beginning until now; on Christ and the evidences
of Christianity; on the Scriptures and especially books
adapted to explain and defend the divine origin and
authority of the Scriptures are aids to spiritual progress which no true disciple of our Lord who has
means and time at his disposal can afford to forego.
The supernatural is so sharply attacked in these days;
so many assaults, disguised and undisguised, are made
on miracles; and so many attempts are put forth to
overturn the very foundations of belief, that it is wise
to know what the brightest minds have to say in support of our faith.

But all large and worthy books on large and
worthy subjects are helpful. "And the books," wrote
Paul to Timothy, — "bring . . . the books." It
ought to be thought a fact of no little significance,
and an authoritative testimony to the value of books,
and a stimulation to the wise and diligent use of
books, that the great Apostle to the Gentiles, when
bolted in behind prison-bars there at Rome, and assured in his own mind that it would not be long before officials charged with the bloody business would
lead him forth to execution, put in an urgent plea
for his books. One is curious to know just what
these books were. There can be no risk in saying
that among the number there must have been the
choicest productions — inspired and uninspired — of
the old Hebrew mind. It is little less certain that in

this small library there were books of classical authors. Repeated references in his sermons and letters leave no doubt that the Apostle was familiar with Stoic modes of thought, and with the sentiment of the Greek poets. But whatever the books were, Paul wanted them; and however brief might be the remaining period of his life he was sure they would bring him light and comfort and courage. God was speaking to his soul in other ways; but He would also speak to his soul through the books. This is one of the open ways through which God has come in on humanity. God did not leave himself without witness in the outer world in that He so created matter and mind that the facts of creation were forced to testify to an everlasting power and divinity. Neither has He left himself without witness in literature. It need not raise the vexed question of inspiration, either as to its purpose or its credential or its variety or its measure, to say God has had so much part and aim, whether the men themselves were conscious of it or not, in the expressions of thought which have been given to the world from century to century by the loftiest minds, that He comes into independent manifestation through these forms of intellectual activity and production, and in this way both confirms our faith in Him and enlarges our conception of His working. To read the Greek Tragedies is to come into a new conviction of the awful fact of retribution for wrong-doing. To read Plato and Cicero and Emerson is to renew strength in the assurance of immortality. To read the biographies of such men as Charlemagne and William of Orange and Oliver Cromwell and George Washington and Abraham Lincoln is to see the divine will in operation in providence and trace the footprints of the Almighty as He moves forward to the accomplishment of His ends amongst the nations. To read Dante and Shakespeare and Milton and Goethe, and their illustrious fellows in song, if the reading be intelligent and sympathetic, is to push back the horizon of the soul and discover new meanings in all the facts of nature and life, and feel constrained to bow with a deeper reverence at the feet of Him whose creative wisdom and energy have wrought out all these wonders. To contemplate a great fact, no matter who has shaped it; to come under the force of a great truth, no matter who has uttered it; to master a great movement in history, no matter whether inside or outside the church, never fails to aid in the development of Christian intelligence and Christian character.

4. *But the way most vital and important of all in which the divine life in man may be developed into the fairest and amplest proportions, is by keeping the soul in living contact with God and cultivating the graces and elements of character which make one most like Christ.*

This means a careful and profound study of the Word of God. Not as literature merely are we thus to study it, but as a source of spiritual light and a channel of divine grace. The Bible is the record of

God's dealings with men. It discloses God in the various aspects of His thought and feeling and intent through the personality of the individual to whom he speaks. It is a revelation to the world of His will, and of the ways so multitudinous in which He draws near and blesses those who obey him, and defeats and overturns those who disregard Him and His laws. The lessons to be learned are both many and precious when we get into close sympathy with the souls on whom God in the olden time laid His burdens, or to whom He whispered His secrets. How it helps us to be told the story of some of the mighty wrestlings of patriarchs and prophets! What could we do without the Psalms to aid us in our self-discoveries and in our bitter confessions and in our joyous ascriptions to the boundless mercy of God? As a guide to right ideas of God, as a ground of confidence in the love of God, as helps in opening out to us the way of life and duty, is there any possible substitute for the Gospel? Could we get along without the Sermon on the Mount, and the Discourse in the Upper Chamber, and the Story of the Crucifixion? The Scriptures are indispensable to spiritual life and growth.

In general a man may know with a good deal of exactness where he is religiously by the place the Bible holds in the routine of his daily life. If it is the newspaper before the Bible; or the magazine, or the novel; if, indeed, it is the best book ever written by an uninspired author before the Bible, the man may take it for granted that his spirituality is not of a very fine or high order, and that the divine life within him needs special nourishing. With a closed Bible, or a Bible opened only fitfully, and read here and there at haphazard, there is not likely to be any advance in thought and apprehension of divine truth, nor any clearer light thrown on the problems of duty. An open Bible is assurance of progress in knowledge and spiritual-mindedness, but a shut Bible is a halt to growth.

This means communion, intimate, loving, habitual, with God in prayer. The prophet speaks of a time when the scattered people of whom he was writing should take root downward and bear fruit upward. No man can ever be well rooted in the divine life, nor eminently fruitful in the divine life, without prayer. With what frequency and earnestness the Psalmist cried out to be taught of God and led in His paths! "Teach me thy way, O Lord." The mind and the heart are to be brought into fresh and living contact with the living God. General Booth evidently puts too little stress on some other means of knowledge and grace, but he is undoubtedly right in getting a man just as soon as possible on his knees before God. In His light they shall see light. Face to face with God the mind acts rapidly, memory and imagination and all the faculties are marvelously quickened; and sin and the consequences of sin are likely to loom before the thought as facts appalling to contemplate. Ideas are flashed upon us, and feelings are stirred within us, when in the attitude of sin-

cere and earnest prayer, of which we might have had
no conception otherwise. This has been the experience of devout men and women throughout the
centuries. In the seclusion of closets God sometimes
approaches wonderfully near to souls. In the light
of closets, when meditation is free and the access of
the Spirit is unhindered, the heart not unfrequently
has startling experiences of self-revelation. In closets, too, heaven seems occasionally to open, and
sights incommunicable salute the vision. No place
is there where the divine life within us can be so
surely and so rapidly developed as in communion
with God.

This means a clean walk. All other means of
maintaining and quickening divine life in the soul
may be employed, but little or nothing will come of
it if there is not a care as to conduct. The heart must
be kept sweet with pure thoughts, and the tongue
unstained with low talk and miserable falsehoods,
and the hands unsoiled by contact with the grime of
sin. God is patient with sinners,—infinitely patient.
There is no one so defiled that He will not help him
into whiteness, if he wishes to be so helped. But
no man can dally with sin; no man can cherish sin;
no man can deliberately plunge down into the vile-
ness of sin, and remain in the fellowship of God.
The divine life in man is begun by giving up sin,
and it is continued and carried on only on condition
that one will consent to be true and open and straightforward. It flourishes only in an atmosphere of
purity.

This means above all else the closest possible identification of the life with the life of Christ. It has already been said that the standard and type of this divine life are found in Christ. He interprets to us what is signified by being made in the image of God, and being a partaker of the divine nature, and being a child of the Heavenly Father. He exhibits to the world the beauty and symmetry of this divine life.

But as Jesus is the measure and illustration of this life, so He is also the source of it. His own words are: "I am . . . the life." "I came that they may have life, and may have it abundantly." This is where we are to start — in Christ. This is where we must abide — in Christ. He is the One we are to follow in all ways of self-denial and loving service — Christ. We are to be so united to Christ, and to have all our motives and aspirations so bound up in Christ, that we can say with the great Apostle: "For me to live is Christ."

This close personal union with Christ lies at the heart of it all. There can be no experience of a genuine divine life, — a life, that is, which is on the plane of the life of the Son of God, and is conformable to the will of God, unless the supplies and inspirations of it come from Christ. One must get his life rooted in Christ as plants are rooted in the earth. One must have his life fed from Christ, as brooks are fed from springs. Admiration of Christ is not enough. It is not enough to be willing to receive

instruction from His lips, and to count Him wise.
It is not enough to be persuaded that He is God
manifest in the flesh. The heart must come under
His quickening power, and the will must answer
affirmatively to His will, and all the channels of the
soul must be open to the inflow of the thought and
energy and spirit of Christ. It must be the realization in fact of the figure of the branches ingrafted
into the vine, and drawing thence the life of their
own life. Moments come to us when we long with
unutterable longing just to be lost in Christ. These
moments are prophetic of what is both desirable and
possible. Moments come to us when we want nothing
so much as to let Christ have His own sweet and unhindered way in us and with us. These moments
are foretastes of the joy which never fails to one who
makes complete surrender to the Lord. Moments
come to us when light from the face of Christ falls
in upon our souls, and the earth is illuminated and
the heavens flame resplendent, and high apocalyptic
visions seem no longer extravagant, and we are exalted into fellowships which are the songs of victory.
These moments are demonstrative of the reality of a
divine life for all who will live it.

One would think it hardly needs to be said, yet it
has been said a great many times in the past, and will
require to be said a great many times in the future,
no doubt, that there is nothing in us, nothing concerning us, which is of so much consequence as falling into line with the will of God, and permitting

His life, so far as may be, to have reproduction in our lives. We win our greatest triumphs, and we realize our loftiest destinies, in the realm of the divine life. To live this life in its fullness is to walk with God, and to know the fellowship of the Son of God, and to enjoy the indwelling of the Holy Spirit, and to advance step by step to the inheritance of the saints in light. This little earthly life comes to an end and disappears; wealth, pleasure and all worldly possessions go with it; but the divine life which is life from God and in God and with God abides forever.

CHRIST THE YEA OF GOD.

In Him is yea. 2 Corinthians 1: 19.

THE special topic suggested by these words, and the topic to which it has seemed to me worth while to invite attention, is: *Christ the Yea of God.*

The story of the circumstances in which the passage before us originated is quickly told. Paul was accused by some of the Corinthian brethren of inconsistency and fickleness. He had been with them once. It was his intention to visit them again, that they might have what he calls a second "benefit" or "favor." But this purpose was changed and another plan was carried out. Advantage was taken of this change of plan to intimate, or, it may be, somewhat more than intimate, that the Apostle was whiffle-minded, and came lightly to his decisions, and as lightly reversed or disregarded them. He was nettled, as any man might well be, by the whispering of things so much to his damage. He was not slow to speak out in his own defense. His defense was to the effect that the accusation was not true. He had not acted from impulse, nor from any low worldly consideration. Though they might think otherwise, his nay was yet nay and his yea was yea.

It was in the course of this explanation, made in

self-defense, that the Apostle had occasion to refer to Christ as the yea of God. He was preaching Christ. It would be a gross ethical inconsistency for him to preach Christ, who was always true to His word, while at the same time he himself was vacillating between yes and no, and saying one thing at one moment, and another thing at another moment, and quite disregarding all his promises. "But as God is faithful, our word toward you is not yea and nay. For the Son of God, Jesus Christ, who was preached among you by us . . . was not yea and nay, but in Him is yea. For how many soever be the promises of God, in Him is the yea."

Of course, it might not follow, either as a matter of fact or of logic, that his preaching of Christ would always hold him steady to the spirit and example of Christ. Nevertheless Paul ventured to think his known loyalty to Christ was such that men could not easily be made to believe him guilty of the moral incongruity of holding Christ forth as the unchanging and unchangeable affirmation of God, while he permitted His Divine example to have no power over his own conduct. One could not be established in Christ without being established in veracity. One could not proclaim Christ without being rebuked and smitten at every utterance, if he should say what he did not mean, or should falter in a manly uprightness and stability. So, he felt sure, men must reason.

With this statement of the occasion there was for bringing this thought forward by the Apostle, and what seemed to him the necessity of it as well, it is now in order to return to it and see what is meant by the assertion that Christ is the yea of God, and what it holds for us. Christ as the Yea of God means two things.

I. *It means in the first place, that in Christ the seal is set to all the promises of God.*

"For how many soever be the promises of God, in Him is the yea."

The presence of Christ in the ranks of our humanity was the full and sweet ratifying of every assurance made by God looking to the restoration of the lost, and the guiding and comforting and upbuilding of the redeemed, from the prophetic moment when the first word of hope was spoken to a guilty and condemned race down to the great hour of the Incarnation. Christ either fulfilled every promise in Himself, or He became the pledge of the fulfillment of every promise which contemplated good to the human race. This is the comforting view which Paul set forth and emphasized in his word to the Romans: "That He might confirm the promises given unto the fathers." Christ was the living So-Be-It with which God rounded out and crowned all He had intimated or declared in the way of awakening expectations through prophets and law-givers and psalmists. Men had only to turn from any reasonable hope the Scriptures had created and look on Christ to find it realized.

II. *Christ as the Yea of God means, in the second place, that He is the affirmation of God.*

Christ manifested God. He set God forth to the reason and the conscience, and made it easier for all souls to apprehend Him and love Him. "The only begotten Son . . . hath declaied Him." "Henceforth ye know Him and have seen Him." "He that hath seen Me hath seen the Father." Christ is the forth-putting of God in the great affirmative elements and attributes of His character. He shows God; He interprets God; He voices God. He is the channel through which the life and light and grace of God flow in upon humanity.

In the opening passage of the Gospel of John, Christ is brought before us in three aspects of His nature. First, He is declared to be God: "The Word was God." Second, He assumes the place and attributes of man: "The Word became flesh and dwelt among us." Third, He is the Revealer of the Father: "No man hath seen God at any time . . . He hath declared Him."

It is in this latter direction that our thought is now moving. In the higher service of revealing the Father, John sets Christ over against Moses and puts what He did to make God, in His essential being, known to the world in sharp contrast to what the great law-giver did. "For the law was given by Moses; grace and truth came by Jesus Christ." The giving of the law was a disclosure of God; but it was not a disclosure so full and tender that it could be said to be a revelation of all that men were capable of apprehending of God. It was a revelation; but it was a revelation preparatory and prophetic; and, like many of the fore-gleams and longings and courageous conjectures found in thoughtful souls lying outside the line of the Chosen People, it looked forward to something yet to come, higher and richer and more satisfactory.

Speaking in general, therefore, it may be said that the Christ did not break in on the world to find it empty of the thought and knowledge of God. In a certain sense men knew God — men everywhere. They knew Him well enough to make them morally accountable for their conduct. "For the invisible things of Him since the creation of the world are clearly seen, being perceived through the things that are made, even His everlasting power and divinity." But in a certain sense men did not know God. "The world through its wisdom," so says the Apostle, again, "knew not God." It did not know Him, that is, in any true and adequate way. It did not know Him rationally and fruitfully. Through sin reason had become darkened and conscience dull. The old revelations were obscure, and God seemed not near, but afar off; not a living personality, but a tradition and a dream.

In his great work on *The Divine Origin of Christianity Indicated by its Historical Effects*, Dr. Storrs says: "There had been points in the experience of various peoples, where natural religion seemed nearly, if not wholly, to touch the level of revelation; where the primitive conception of God had been so completely worthy and high that the subsequent descent from it seems almost incredible.''

This distinguished author does not attempt to explain these high, primitive conceptions of God, which are discoverable in peoples other than the Hebrews, though he admits and indorses the claim. His inclination is to think man has an innate sense of God, which sense is implied in his constant consciousness of dependence and also of obligation. Both these feelings point to a Power above him and open the way for any approaches God may wish to make to the souls of His earthly children.

But the fact of this universal consciousness of God is all that now concerns us. Theism — monotheism — appears to have been an original and universal conception in the primitive religions of mankind. At the fountain-heads of life, before the streams had been corrupted by wrong doing and idle speculation, men felt or reasoned their way into the thought of God, and God was acknowledged.

The Old Testament makes it clear that along one line of descent from the original ancestors of mankind, and for centuries upon centuries, a well-defined and lofty idea of God was maintained. Abel, Noah, Abraham, Moses, Samuel, David, Isaiah, Daniel, Malachi, John the Baptist were exponents, each in his own way, of views of God, which were creditable alike to their heads and hearts. God in the personality of His being, in His essential oneness, in the infinitude and sovereignty of His power, and the eter-

nity of His existence, as well as in certain aspects of
His love and care, was domesticated and cherished
in the thought of the Hebrew mind.

Pains must be taken not to underestimate what
was known of God before Christ came to make the
larger and clearer revelation. Men who have points
to score are in danger of not giving sufficient credit
to the old knowledge. In His natural attributes, and
in some phases of His moral attributes, there was
not much to be desired, to make the conception of
God, as entertained by the best and most devout souls
among His ancient people, elevated and satisfactory.
Some of the statements concerning the greatness
and wisdom and majesty and might of God found
in Genesis and Job, in the Psalms and Prophets,
challenge rivalry. "In the beginning God created
the heavens and the earth" is a statement at once and
a tribute which admit of no improvement.

At the same time, the disclosure which Jesus
Christ made of God — the interpretation which He
gave of the character of God, — was so much in advance, though in some particulars projected along
the same lines with which the best spirits were familiar, and supplemental of anything the world had
ever known before, that it might be truly said: "No
man hath seen God at any time; the only begotten
Son which is in the bosom of the Father, He hath
revealed Him."

But let us deal more specifically with the service
rendered by our Lord in this sphere.

1.   *To begin with, Christ revived and restored God to the place in the thoughts of men He had once held, but out from which He had fallen through the degeneration of moral life in the nations.*

The conception of God, as once cherished by intelligent and reverent souls, not only outside but inside the Jewish nationality, had lost a large part of its vital force. There was no longer any living pulse in it. The knowledge of God, as the most knew Him, was a dead knowledge,— an empty and mocking tradition. There are hardly any pages in history so sad as those which record the lapse of men from faith in God, and the consequent decay of conscience and righteousness, and the awful plunge downward into sensuality. The idea of God had become so dwarfed and debased in the common apprehension, that multitudes amongst the foremost people of the globe did not hesitate to ascribe to Him, or to the countless deities into which they divided the one Supreme Being, the same appetites and passions and lusts which had control in their own lives. They first degraded themselves, and then they degraded God.

The coming of Christ was like the sudden bursting of a glorious sunrise upon a world which had somehow forgotten to turn its face to the day, and was weltering in a darkness which was all the time growing deeper and deeper. Had not Christ appeared when He did, with a revelation of God which was fresh and vital and more commanding than any ever before made, it is difficult to see how the nations, one

and all, could have kept from drifting back into utter
barbarism, or rotting down into a loathsome mass.
Here and there one might come upon an exception;
but in the popular thought, and in the ruling thought,
there was no God. It was atheism. It was panthe-
ism. It was polytheism. To avow any faith, in
most quarters of the civilized world, was to become
a target for the shafts of ridicule. Christ re-created
a conception of God under the ribs of moral and
spiritual death. He made men sensible once more
of the beating of the Divine heart.

2. *Further than this, as has been hinted already, Christ took men forward into new thoughts
of God.*

If we may so speak, Christ unfolded God to men;
though, perhaps, it would be better to say that He
unfolded Himself to men, and in the unfolding of
Himself men saw God. This is a distinction which
belongs to Christianity, and differentiates it from all
other religions. Moses, for instance, was trained and
inspired of God to deliver a people from bondage,
and organize them into a nation, and to disclose to
them the law under which they should live. He
spoke as he had been spoken to, and revealed that
which had been revealed to him. Nothing was self-
originated; it was all from God. But we never
think of Christ as inspired in any such sense as this.
He simply stands there, and utters His word, and
does His deed, and straightway the impression seizes
us that we are witnessing a manifestation of God.

Dr. Schaff, in a very suggestive paragraph, puts forward the thought that the best reason discoverable for calling Christ the Logos — the Word — is that He is the revealer and interpreter of God in all which relates to our salvation. John, he adds, "places the supreme dignity of Christ, as the Eternal Word, the author of the world, the giver of life and light, the fountain of grace and truth, the only perfect expounder of God, at the head of his gospel, because without this dignity Christianity would sink to a position of merely relative superiority to other religions, instead of being the absolute and, therefore, the final religion for all mankind." In our Christianity we have, not an evolution from Judaism, but a fresh and advance revelation of God. In beholding Christ, beams of a supernatural light flash upon us, and we have a new and higher sense of the character of God.

Passing from this general statement to particulars, it is to be said that we have not followed Christ the full length to which He went in taking men over into a new conception of the nature of God, until we have observed and emphasized the unprecedented stress He laid on the Divine love, and the way, wholly original, in which He demonstrated that the compassion of God is measureless and flows out to mankind in boundless currents.

That God is pure is one of the early ideas of religion. This idea, as we have seen, was largely lost out of the conceptions of men. But it was amongst the early ideas of God. Almost every page of the

Old Testament flashes with the Divine holiness. It is in the law, the ceremonies, the promises, the approbations, the punishments, and whatever else there is to show forth the character of the Supreme Being. This idea Jesus illustrated and enforced. Purity, righteousness, holiness were great words with our Lord. "Blessed are the pure in heart, for they shall see God."

Not with this idea, however, did He stop. While constantly magnifying holiness, as in the Sermon on the Mount, and in other discourses, by showing how interior, how penetrating, how wide-sweeping are all the commandments, He also showed how the holiness of God is warmed and illuminated by a wealth of affection in the Divine heart, of which men had only the vaguest notion until the Son of God became incarnate, and set this wealth of loving interest forth on the lip and in the life. Not till Christ came, and in His own personality made the world see and feel it, was there ever any adequate comprehension of the length and breadth and height and depth of the love of God. Prophets had said it, psalmists had sung it, devout souls had felt it, but the overwhelming demonstration of it awaited the matchless scene of the Son of God dying on the Cross of Calvary.

Take this word "Father"— our "Heavenly Father." Max Mueller has said that he finds "Heavenly Father" to be a name for God among all the original Aryan peoples, and that he traces the name to the ancient mythologies of India, Greece, Italy and

Germany. But it has been shown that the word "Father" did not mean in this early use what it came to mean under Christian teaching. To quote once more the words of an authority so eminent as Dr. Storrs: "It did not imply, whatever under Stoicism it did, a generative paternity. It did not in the least imply affectionate paternity. It represented supremacy only; was applied by poets to those whom they honored; by slaves and clients to masters and patrons. The idea it contained when applied to the gods was of paramount authority — superlative dignity. But Christianity shows the Fatherhood of God, in His spirit of love as well as in His authorship of finite intelligence, extending to all who are born of His life, and becoming intense toward those who seek moral fellowship with Him. To them He gives gifts, according to this conception of things, which the mind of the world had wholly failed to attribute to Him, or to conceive possible, until it was exalted and instructed by Jesus — the gift of His own thought not only, but of His essential and renovating spiritual power."

To the same effect is Bishop Lightfoot. Speaking of the use of the word "Father" by the Stoics in such sublime hymns as Cleanthes has left us, where we come upon the expressions, "Thine Offspring are We," "Do Thou, Father," and others like them, he says: "If these words might be accepted in their first and obvious meaning, we could hardly wish for any more sublime and devout expressions of the creature to his Creator and Father. But a reference to the doctrinal teaching of this school dispels the splendid illusion. Stoic dogma empties Stoic hymnology of half its sublimity and more than half its devoutness. This father in heaven, we learn, is no personal being, all righteous and all holy, of whose loving care the purest love of an earthly parent is but a shadowy counterfeit. He — or It — is only another name for Nature, for necessity, for fate, for the universe. Just in proportion as this theological doctrine of the school is realized, does its liturgical language appear forced and unnatural. Terms derived from human relationships are confessedly very feeble and inadequate at best to express the person and attributes of God; but only a mind prepared by an artificial training could use such language as I have quoted with the meaning which it is intended to bear. To simple people it would be impossible to address fate, or necessity, or universal nature, as a father, or to express toward it feelings of filial obedience and love." Does not the thought grow upon us that he, and he only, who has seen Jesus Christ hath seen the Father?

It is a vast addition and precious above price — this which has been made to the stores of the moral and spiritual wealth of mankind by the new nearness into which the Father has been brought to all discerning souls by the disclosures of the Son of God. In a sense only dimly and hesitatingly suspected until God became manifest in the person of His Son, and the Son interpreted Him to the world, was it discovered that God is immanent in all facts — transcendent, but still immanent — and in all laws and in all life; and that He is immanent to instruct, and to guard, and to guide, and to purify, and to save unto the uttermost all who come unto Him through Christ. He is immanent in love.

a. In this view of Christ as the Yea of God, or the seal of all His promises and the affirmation of His thought and character, there is something assured and positive to which we can cling.

Christ is not a guess. He is not a vague uncertainty. He is not a fascinating but illusive dream. He is a teacher sent of God, — sent to tell us of God, to open the way to God. Through Him God comes to us, and pours His light and love in upon our souls; and we have rest in sure and everlasting verity. Our hands find their way into God's hand, and we hold and are held.

One of the most suggestive and stirring sections to be found in the writings of Thomas Carlyle is that in "Sartor Resartus," in which he throws out his thoughts under the successive headings, in three successive chapters, of *The Everlasting No, Center of Indifference, The Everlasting Yea.*

It is the story of a struggling soul's experience, told as only this great Scotchman would be likely to tell it, when first fairly confronted with the problem of its own existence, and feeling under the bonds of its own being to come to some sort of rational and definite conclusion about the matter. The first impulse was, of course, to question. Then, when the answers to these questions did not come fast enough, or were not satisfactory, the impulse was to deny. Along this path the descent was sure, if not easy, down into the depths of utter negation.

But the point of special interest and pertinacy is that after all the beating back and forth with questions of doubt and denial; after all the settling down into the determination to fret no more over the high concerns, but to lie still, like a poor baffled bird within the bars of its cage, and let things turn out as they might, and destiny be what it would, there are yet impulses within the soul, or influences without the soul, or both coöperant, which force one up and out of his mood of negation, and out of his mood of indifference, and drive him on, provided the reason and conscience are not wholly thwarted, until he has standing on the high tableland where the earth is solid beneath his feet, and the sky is clear over his head, and he has knowledge — living, personal, sweet — of Him who is behind all the stars, and who is also not far from any one of His earthly children.

This is a lesson of vast moment. With all his mental vagaries and shortcomings, Carlyle had the wit to see that this universe has truth at the core of it, and he kept on saying so to the end. Men might fling out their objections into the face of shining worlds, and close their ears against all voices from afar, and shut their eyes against flaming visions; but it would amount to nothing. No soul, so this man felt; and so millions on millions of this race of ours have found, can rest in an attitude of negation and denial. No soul can feed itself into strength and beauty and peace on negation and denial. The region where the answer to every question is No, is not a region of life, but of moral and spiritual death. Men cannot build on Nay. If they build at all, build any sort of enduring structure, it must be on Yea. We are in a universe of affirmations. Yea is written everywhere across earth and sky. The world under our feet is Yea. The sun, flooding all our atmosphere with light, and kissing every valley and plain and hillside into beauty, is Yea. The stars, circling in their orbits and greeting each other across the spaces, are Yea. The human soul, made for truth and made for life, is Yea. God over all and in all is Yea. As face answereth to face, so the cry of the soul for yea is answered by the yea of God in Christ. In Him is Yea, and because He is Yea we can rest in Him forever.

b. In this view of Christ, too, as the yea of God, or the seal of all His promises and the affirmation of His thought and character, there is something clear and positive and helpful for us to commend to others.

Not only is God so certified to us in Christ that we can build the structure of our immortal hopes on Him; but God is so certified to us in Christ that we can take Him and put Him under souls, and make Him the foundation, sure and immovable, of their immortal hopes. God in Christ is as clear as the sun-light, and as self-demonstrative, and we can speak of Him with as much assurance. God in Christ is as positive as the law of gravitation, and we can talk of Him and commend Him with all the confidence with which scientists speak of the mysterious force which holds the globe in compactness, and keeps stars and systems of stars moving on in majestic harmony. God in Christ is eternal truth.

This is what men want. It is not alone what they need, but what they want and will welcome. At times it does not seem so; but in any large generalization it will be discovered that men desire something clear, something positive, something vital, something which will be light to darkened souls, and bread to hungry souls, and water to thirsty souls, and life to souls dead in trespasses and sins. In the long run it will be found that what men have an ear for is not the nay of doubt, but the yea of God. Fancies, no matter how beautiful, conjectures, no matter how plausible, vagaries, speculations, denials, negations, are not the materials with which souls are built up into solid and symmetrical proportions. It is not the nay of men, but the yea of God with which human hearts are to be purified and filled with nobler aspirations, and with which human society is to be renewed and exalted to its high estate. It may be entertaining, but there is no such foolish beating of the air as standing in pulpits and sawing back and forth at guesses and criticisms and empty specula-

tions.   God in Christ is living, breathing truth. God
in Christ is the light of the world, because He is the
light of individual souls.

No man who has ever read the Gospels with a half-
open eye can have failed to see how positive Christ
was in all His preaching. He was a yea, and not a nay
preacher.   He put forth certainties, and not doubts.
God, the heavenly Father — what a verity He was
to the Son of God! Our sinfulness — was there ever
any question about it in the speech of Jesus? Our
peril in consequence of our sinfulness — what word
ever fell from the lips of the Great Teacher to warrant one in thinking he might go, all unconcerned,
masquerading and full of frolic, out into eternity?
The necessity of being born again — did He not say
it even to the circumspect and reputable Nicodemus?
The love of God full, free, abounding, — did He not
dwell on it and magnify it from beginning to end?
Truth to endure forever; justice at the heart of things;
divine compassion enfolding the race like an atmosphere and holding the world in its arms; life, death,
heaven, hell, judgment, responsibility, duty; how to
please God; how to develop the image of God in which
we were made; how to realize the end of our being
and make sure of heirship to the everlasting inheritance — these were the themes of Jesus. Not the un-
certainties, but the certainties.

On this basis it is worth while to preach and to list-
en to preaching.   For what music it makes for the
heart, bewildered and sore distressed, when this In-

carnate Yea of God answers back with a yes which
has no tone of equivocation or misgiving in it to each
eager question sent up to Him! Have we a Father
in heaven who knows us, who loves us, who is
thoughtful of us and who broods over us in the tenderness of a Divine pity? Yea. May we, weak
and finite as we are, come into a sense of sonship
and know this heavenly Father, and walk in His
blessed fellowship? Yea. If one has wandered afar
and has only a bruised and darkened and defiled soul,
is there any way in which he may return to loyalty,
and find purity and peace and joy once more? Yea.
After the struggle is all over and one has served this
Divine Master to the best of his ability, is there for
him, — not in virtue of his own merit, but through
the infinite riches of the grace of God in Christ
Jesus, — is there for him a life out beyond, ampler,
better, in every way more glorious than this earthly
life, to be lived in the open presence of Him who
redeemed us to Himself? Yea. It is all yea. The
incarnation is yea; the teaching is yea; the cross is
yea; the resurrection is yea; the Holy Spirit is yea;
the promises are yea; the hopes are yea; the beckon-
ing splendors are yea; the rewards are yea. Trusting
in Jesus and moving forward hand in hand with
Him, we come in His own wise time to the crowning
yea of all where we stand face to face with God, and
have experience of the joys and fellowships and glories of the kingdom from which we go no more out
forever.

AWAKING TO RIGHTEOUSNESS.

Awake up righteously, and sin not; for some have no knowledge of God. 1 Cor. 15:34.

THIS is the new version. In substance it does not differ from the old, which rings out with its more familiar and somewhat sharper watch-cry: "Awake to righteousness." But whatever the form, the meaning is the same, and there is no escaping it. From the whole passage it is perfectly evident that what the Apostle desires is to arouse men to a new and clearer moral discernment, and to set them forward into a new and higher moral condition. There are men who are asleep, so Paul conceives it, to right things. He means to have them awakened out of their sleep, — stirred and shaken, if need be, till they open their eyes to the light, and their lives are brought under the power of truth and goodness and purity, and their whole being stands for what God approves.

A pertinent exhortation back in old Corinth eighteen hundred years ago, it is still, here and everywhere, a pertinent exhortation; and my voice this morning is to be pitched to the same key: *Awaking to righteousness*.

Passing at once to the business in hand suggested by this theme,

I. *It is to be observed, in the first place, as a fact of profound significance that all the disclosures of God which are made to us, and all the movements of God in upon the world and among men which we can discover, are steadily and stoutly in the direction of righteousness.*

Righteousness is God's wish concerning us. In trying to be righteous we come into accord with the will of God, and we fall into line with the vast array of moral forces which are abroad in the universe.

The studies and conclusions of the late Matthew Arnold are not without their value here. His well known definition of God is: "The Power, not ourselves, which makes for righteousness." To me this has never seemed a satisfactory definition, but it has the merit of admitting the conception of righteousness to be fundamental to the nature of God, and also the uniform tendency to righteousness which there is in all the out-goings of God.

He says further: "The word 'righteousness' is the master word of the Old Testament. 'Keep judgment, and do righteousness.' 'Cease to do evil, learn to do well.' 'Offer the sacrifice, not of victims and ceremonies, but of righteousness.'"

He adds to this: "The great concern of the New Testament is likewise righteousness; but righteousness reached through particular means by the power of Christ." A sentence which sums up the New Testament; so he avows,"and assigns the ground whereon the Christian Church stands . . . is this: 'Let

every one that nameth the Name of Christ depart
from iniquity.'"

According to Mr. Arnold's estimate, conduct is
three-fourths of life; the object of religion is conduct, and conduct such as meets the requirements
of the Bible, is but another name for righteousness.

As already intimated, this is imperfect teaching. It
is vague and illusive. It is not like the instruction of
Jesus — not like it either in matter or tone. It is not
fitted to stir men out of their moral stupors, like the
clear ringing words of Moses and Isaiah and Paul.
Still it is much to have the frank admission, and even
the claim, of a man who furnishes not a little of the
stock in trade of our small dealers in doubt that the
Bible, both in its revelation of God and in the whole
sweep of its precepts, lays such tremendous stress on
righteousness. He seems to advance a step and
clinch this view of the matter by saying he supposes
nobody will deny that the Old Testament is filled
with the word and thought of righteousness.

Whether denied or not, this is the fact. It is the
fact of the Old Testament, and it is the fact of
the New Testament. The uniform pressure of
the Word of God is toward pure hearts and clean
hands. Study the Decalogue, — the core and aim
of all the Commandments will be found to be righteousness. Study the words of Prophets and Apostles;
it is the same, — they all look forward to righteousness. Providence, in the long run, with the history
and destiny of nations for its letters, spells out right-

eousness. The Spirit convicts of sin and leads on by
way of truth into righteousness. The moral law and
the moral sense meet in a common approval of righteousness. The old-time view was: "Lord, who shall
sojourn in thy tabernacle? Who shall dwell in thy
holy hill? He that walketh uprightly, and worketh
righteousness, and speaketh truth in his heart." The
new time and everlasting view is: "Not every one
that saith unto me, Lord, Lord, shall enter into the
kingdom of heaven, but he that doeth the will of my
Father which is in heaven." From beginning to end,
and all through, both in letter and in spirit, it is —
God intent on righteousness.

This much, then, is clear and beyond gainsaying.
The inmost aim of God, the whole sweep of the divine influence, the whole sweep of the divine laws,
are toward an enduring moral rectitude. God
is pitiful. The Christ was foretold to be one who would
not break the bruised reed, nor quench the smoking
flax. But if He bends down tenderly over the err-
ing, as He does, it is that He may lift them up and
set them right. If He feels infinite compassion for
the impure, as He does, it is that He may reach their
hearts with the breath of the Spirit and cleanse them
into whiteness. If He goes out lovingly after wrong-
doers, as He does, it is that He may persuade them
to turn from their iniquities to holiness. The intent
of God — an intent so plain that nobody can well miss
it — is to induce men, as Daniel significantly puts
it, "to break off their sins by righteousness."

Not by any searching can we find out God unto perfection. He is higher than all heights, deeper than all depths. At the same time it is impossible to get the least hint of God without discovering that iniquity and uncleanness offend Him, while right conduct, cultivated and carried on till it has become crystallized into pure and lofty character, gives Him supreme satisfaction. "Be ye holy, for I am holy." Be the feelings of God toward the unrighteous what they may; be the consequences of breaking away from righteousness what they may; be the methods of getting back into righteousness what they may; and there can be little room for doubt on any of these questions; still the thing which suits God, — which has the divine affirmation on it, and which God wants all men everywhere to illustrate, is righteousness.

II. *Turning the subject about and looking at it now from our human standpoint, it may be said, as a second consideration of weight, that our own welfare and efficiency demand a large measure of righteousness.*

As has just been seen, a religion which is worth anything in God's sight must be a religion which registers itself in righteousness. It is exactly so with men. A religion to be of any solace to our own hearts, or of any value and force in the estimation of the world, must be a religion which registers itself in righteousness. Men refuse to be swayed by a faith which, though it bring the knees down in devout adoration, does not relax the selfish grip of the hand; which, though it roll from the lips in the most resonant tones, or be chanted with the most artistic grace of delicate organ notes, does not restrain the tongue from lying, nor keep back the feet from paths of wickedness. Faith, apart from works, so we are told, is dead. Being dead, men say, and they ought to say: Let the thing be buried. A faith which does not put itself forward, as by a kind of seed-instinct, into feelings and thoughts of righteousness, and into righteous conduct, is a delusion and a snare. To the men who hold it, and to the world at large, this kind of faith is altogether mischievous. Nothing does so much to furnish plausible excuses to men who are conscious of their wrong attitudes and their ill-desert, but who are yet reluctant to move forward into right relations with God, as a hollow faith. Nothing does so much to warrant candid men in questioning whether all religion be not an empty farce and superstition.

To be somewhat more definite in the statement of the case:

1. *There is need of righteousness as against a mere dead orthodoxy.*

It is a misfortune when things which naturally belong together have to be set over against each other in sharp contrast. It would be difficult to put too much emphasis on the importance of right views. Neither in political nor religious spheres do men gather grapes of thorns. The Apostle was neither beating the air, nor expending his energy on an insignificant matter, when he urged the maintenance of the pattern of sound words. Nevertheless it does not follow from this that all right views will fructify in right lives, and that there never will be any break in the connection between correct opinions and correct conduct.

It was the same seed which the sower held in his hand and scattered broadcast. But it was only the seed which fell into good ground which brought forth fruit. If it had not been good seed it would not have borne fruit, even in good ground. Yet, being good seed, it was scattered all in vain on the wayside, in the stony places, and among thorns. The fault was not in the seed; the seed was just what it ought to have been; the fault was that there was no right reception of it, or right cultivation. The seed was good, still it came to nothing.

There is more or less of orthodoxy which never becomes righteousness. It is orthodoxy, and as such it is to be upheld and cherished; but right in theory, it comes to nothing right in the life. This is the open shame of it. There is little heresy so fatally harmful. Heresy in opinion is bad. Sooner or later, as was stated a little back, whether in philosophy or statesmanship or religion, it will come to disastrous explosion. But the heresy of dishonesty; the heresy of meanness; the heresy which shields itself from meeting just obligations by quibbles which would make a shyster blush; the heresy which mounts the housetop and bawls, "Lord, Lord," and yet lends the brain to the cunning schemes of the devil, and permits the hand to do the devil's service, and the feet to run on the devil's errands, — what shall be said of men guilty of this sort of heresy? Just what Jesus said: "Woe unto you, scribes and Pharisees, hypocrites, for ye tithe mint and anise and cummin, and have left undone the weightier matters of the law, judgment and mercy and faith; but these ye ought to have done, and not to have left the other undone."

It is my constant desire that men believe. I want them to believe sincerely and earnestly and stoutly. To that end with whatever power belongs to me I am steadily working. To me it seems clear that there are sufficient grounds on which to base a faith of this sort in all the fundamental doctrines of the Word of God. For all this it is not to be forgotten, that even devils may believe, and may believe to the point of trembling, and yet be devils still. Just as fast and just as far as faith gets on into faithfulness, and right views take form in right living, shall we realize God's thought concerning us, or be in a condition to make our views effective, and to render the best service to all good causes in our day and generation. True believing tends to true living, but true living is the indispensable seal of true believing.

2. *In the second place, it is to be righteousness as against mere emotion.*

Here again the task is an ungracious one. For one does not wish even to seem to speak in disparagement of religious feeling. Warmth is good. Religion has been defined to be morality touched with emotion. If morality be thought of as conformity to the law of God, the definition is not far out of the way. Religion is quite likely to lose some of its force, and much of its beauty and attractiveness, if it has no pulse of feeling in it. We all like the severe accuracy of the multiplication table; we also like the freshness and fragrance and charming symmetry of the rose. The sun knows how to give out both light and heat. We want both. The brook is none the less useful in turning mills because it sings as it flows. Birds would not be birds if they did not yield to their own impulses of delight, and fill the air with their morning melodies. Religion appeals to the heart. If it be genuine it kindles the heart, quickens all the sensibilities, and puts an unwonted glow into the speech.

But to feel religious emotion, and, within due limitations, to give expression to religious emotions is one thing. To feel religious emotion, and to go soaring off on the wings of religious rapture, without any apparent appreciation of the obligations and duties of religion, is quite another thing. It is this latter which is reprehensible. We want emotion; but we do not want it to be all gush and no principle, all sentiment and no obedience. To revel in the poetry of religious feeling, and to forget all about the cup of cold water to the thirsty, is to mock the teaching of the Master.

Little danger is there of pressing this distinction

too urgently. There is a time for tears. There is a time to let the heart speak right out of its own rich experience. There is a time, not only to yield to it, but to help swell the tide of holy enthusiasm. Miriam was not afraid to sing her song of triumph. The Psalmist was not afraid to let the chord of his own heart respond freely to the touches of inspiration. Paul was not afraid to tell of dreams and visions and extraordinary exaltations of soul. It is only when all the energies are expended in these direc- tions, and much is felt and nothing is done, that emo- tion becomes offensive. The world has no fancy for a religion which runs all to mouth.   It is not safe to put confidence in religion, unless the moral side keeps pace with the emotional side, and an unyielding stress is laid on righteousness.

Madame Roland, on her way to the guillotine, lifted her eyes to the ugly instrument of death, and ex- claimed: "O Liberty, what crimes have been com- mitted in thy name!" Often one cannot help appropriating the words, and crying out: "O Relig- ion, what inconsistencies and wrongs and horrid in- iquities have been committed in thy name!" The corrective is to lay emphasis on righteousness, and to see to it that pious feelings are not divorced from holy acts. With an eminent fitness some one has called these emotional Christians the "sensitive plants" of the church. They turn this way and that in response to every influence which plays upon them, and they are easily wrought up into spasms of surface sympathy; but they bear little fruit. What they need is to be established in the truth and habit of righteousness.

3. *In the third place it is to be righteousness as against mere worldly policies and methods.*

This is the same as saying it is to be righteousness after the divine standard, and not a righteousness made up of the shreds and patches of the hour's latest conceit. An old writer, of distinction in his day, has said the laws of men are not our rule. "Men make laws," so he tells us, "as tailors do garments — to fit the crooked bodies they serve for." Men make laws to suit the humors of the people who are to be governed by these laws. "It is God's prerogative," he adds, "to give law to the conscience. Human laws are good to establish converse with men; but too short to establish communion with God. Therefore we must consult with the rule which is the law of the Lord, if we would not come short of true blessedness."

It cannot be too early and definitely settled that there is but one measure of righteousness for us. The world may have a thousand standards; Christian men can have but one, and by that one they must abide. No matter how others buy and sell; no matter how others fall into the currents of the world in seeking promotion and happiness; no matter how others shrink back when burdens are to be borne, and fidelity to truth means loss and pain; those of us who believe in God and are trying to do the will of God, are to be Daniels in integrity, and to hold fast our uprightness whatever foes conspire and whatever perils threaten. There are never wanting those who are ready to weave webs of sophistry with which to entangle our judgment, and to sing songs fitted to lull the conscience into easy acquiescence with evil suggestions: "What's the harm?" and "What's the harm?" But we must remember it is God with whom our account lies, and stand like a rock.

This, then, is to be the stamp of our righteousness. Righteousness like this will give us some real effectiveness and make our influence a positive force for good. In other words, if our righteousness is vital instead of being a bundle of mere lifeless opinions — no matter how correct in form; if our righteousness is practical, and does not exhaust itself in the vaporings of transient emotion and tender effervescence; if our righteousness has primary reference to God and seeks to adjust itself to the laws and commandments of God rather than to echo ideas and follow methods which happen to be current in fashionable circles, and in the marts of trade; and so is a genuine righteousness, and not an empty similitude of righteousness, there will be untold good in it for ourselves and for the world.

For this kind of righteousness is character, and character always counts. If it be known that a man will not lie, nor cheat, nor meanly falter, nor evade any responsibility which falls to his lot; but, wherever he is put, whether in a bank or store, whether in the management of a large estate or a great corporation, whether in executive office or legislative hall or on the bench, will be square and clean and manly, he will be sure to be a positive moral force. These are the men who preserve and foster the moral sense of a community, and who keep the wheels of civilization moving forward on the lines of a true progress.

It is men after this type, too, who are invaluable to a city or a state. Take the men of unimpeachable moral character and of high moral standards and methods out of a community, and though there may be many millionaires left, and many men left competent to push great material enterprises to successful issues, and men of genius to utter thoughts, and men of fashion to keep the surface of life gay and festive, the tendency, and the increasing tendency, in society will be back toward shallowness and barbarism. The moral element is the element preservative of all other elements in the individual and the nation.

It is common for us to say: "This man has large capacity for public affairs; how much we owe to him!" True. "This man has rare business foresight and skill; how much we owe to him!" True again. But how rarely does it occur to us to say: "This man has delicate moral instincts, an integrity which is never misled, nor caught in the cunning traps of hood-winking casuists; how much we owe to *him!*" Yes, to *him*, indeed. For men of this cast, in virtue of their simple-being, lift homes and social circles and the manner of conducting business and people and all humanity nearer to God. What do we read? Was it for lack of orators like Demosthenes and Webster to illuminate great subjects and to stir vast masses at will that the city was swept out of existence? Was it for lack of painters like Raphael and Guido Reni to lay their colors on canvas or fling them up against ceilings in forms of immortal beauty? Was it for lack of sculptors like Michael Angelo or Thorwaldsen to chisel figures out of rough marble quarries so much like the human that the perpetual wonder is they do not speak? Was it for want of capitalists to undertake important public improvements and push them on to a consummation in which all the citizens should take a justifiable pride? Not at all. It was for lack of *a few righteous men* that Sodom was destroyed.

Let us have men of skill; men of enterprise; explorers, inventors, tradesmen, manufacturers; let us have men who are not daunted by such stupendous undertakings as ocean telegraphs, and Mount Cenis tunnels, and Suez and Nicaragua canals, and Rocky Mountain railroads, and Brooklyn bridges. But above all let us have men who know how to be righteous, and who esteem righteousness, and who infuse the fine aroma of righteousness all abroad, and who put the stamp of righteousness on everything they touch.

There is no cry of the hour so imperative as for men of righteousness. The vices of Corinth abound still. The human nature of the old Greek is the human nature of the Saxon and the Celt. The canker of corruption which consumed ancient nations, threatens modern nations, and it will be just as fatal unless arrested. Men are sowing to the wind; the harvest will be whirlwind. The sad and fatal carnival of lying and stealing and forgery and drunkenness and robbery and arson and licentiousness and murder goes on, and the woe of wickedness is everywhere. The boundary lines of nations are made the bulwark of scamps and scoundrels; and men with the brand of guilt on their foreheads flee abroad, that under the shelter of foreign flags they may defy the laws they have broken at home, and feast on their ill-gotten gains. Mobs take the law into their own hands, and irresponsible leaders overawe the regularly constituted authorities, and check the currents of industry at their pleasure. Surely it is a time for making protests in the interest of virtue, and boldly exalting the banner of righteousness.

We need not shut our eyes to other demands and duties. Let the work of teaching go on. Let knowledge grow from more to more. Let the singers sing their songs and the artists reproduce their lofty thoughts on canvas, in poems, in sculpture and in beautiful and impressive material structures. Let the historians uncover and disclose the majestic past. Let the scientists unlock the mysteries of nature, and bring out the secrets which stars and lilies and rocks and water-drops and fire-mist hold in their jealous

keeping.   Let men sow and reap; buy and sell; sail
the seas and lakes and rivers; keep plane and trowel
and loom and forge in motion; subdue forests, and
rear houses, and make laws, and perform all the
functions of a cultivated and energetic people.   Still
so long as there is a vestige left of injustice and immorality and crime, there must be an incessant iter-
ation of the grand old word — *Righteousness.*

III.   *Our view, however, is not complete, but is
still lacking in development at a most vital point until
it is added, that, as the sense of the obligation and
the habit of righteousness disappear when God drops
out of mind, so the way to restore the sense of the
obligation and the habit of righteousness is to acquaint men with God, and bring them into loyalty
to the will of God.*

Observe the language of the passage: "Awake
up righteously and sin not; *for some have no knowledge of God.*"

Right there lies the open secret of the moral stu-
pidity out of which men are to be aroused, and the
sin from which they are to be turned, — they have
ceased to know God in any true and living way.   God
is not in all their thoughts.   He has been ruled out
and dismissed.

Paul's idea was that there is not only an intimate
but a vital relation between a knowledge of God and
true morals.   In this he was surely right.   A true
ethic has its root in a true view of God.   Attempt to
get a motive for moral conduct, or a sanction for

moral conduct, in anything short of the Infinite Reason, and sooner or later the stress of responsibility for right conduct will cease to be felt, and men instead of saying: "We ought," will be saying: "We wish," or "We will." Blind men, that is, to God, divorce men from a sense of obligation to do the will of God, and the door to all sorts of delinquencies and vices swings wide open. Men will soon be going in and out, indulging passions and appetites, betraying innocence, committing wrongs, and working a thousand mischiefs, with only the slightest compunction.

If, therefore, righteousness is to be secured and developed and illustrated, it is to be by turning about and retracing the paths along which men have walked in becoming lost to righteousness. There will be no clear perception of moral distinctions, and no deep and irresistible conviction of moral obligations, till these distinctions are seen in the light of the face of God, and these obligations are felt to be none other than the pressure of the finger of God.

For this knowledge of God, personal, practical, there is no possible substitute. In some quarters it is fashionable to lay great stress on art, as though galleries opulent in fine pictures and exquisite statuary were pledges of purity. But is history so easily forgotten? When and where did art achieve any such desirable results? Was it in Athens? Athens had art, but where was the purity? Recall how licentiousness thrives under the very eves of the rarest art col-

lections in Europe.   Paris and Vienna would not be
what they are, were it in the power of art to elevate
and conserve the morals of a people.   In some quarters learning is looked upon as an adequate remedy
for existing and threatening evils.   It would be difficult to overestimate the importance of universal education.   But it is not in learning to insure righteousness.   Neither is it in the wisest political economics.
Neither is it in the accumulation of vast wealth, especially if the wealth, as the experience of ages shows
is likely to be the case, becomes unequally distributed.
Laws may be made as wholesome as possible, and
still it is not in laws.   By no one of these methods,
nor by all of them together, are men and communities of men held to the white line of a lofty and enduring righteousness.

   Given the indispensable condition of a disposition
to recognize God, and to obey God, and all these
things help.   Pictures help.   Music helps.   Good
theories of government help.   Good laws help.
Wealth, to flow out freely in the direction of public
improvement and general beneficence, helps immensely.

   But when men permit God to drift away out of
their thoughts, and no more questions are asked
about the will of God, and no more apprehensions
are felt about the consequences of disobeying God,
it will not be long before the consciences of men will
become drowsy and flabby, and righteousness will
be overthrown in the street.   It is root and fruit.

The tap-root of righteousness runs back to God. If the root be cut, or in any way disconnected, righteousness will wither and die.

This makes the whole business plain. The way to promote righteousness is to promote a knowledge of God. As righteousness is disintegrated and destroyed in the individual, and through the individual in the state, by paralyzing the faith of man in God; so righteousness is secured and built up by bringing men under the sweet and wholesome constraint of the Divine Will. He who is undermining the confidence of men in a divine source of authority, and in a divine order of things in the world, whether in private conversation or on the platform, or through tracts and editorials and books, is fitting them to run off, in no long time, into innumerable crimes and vices and cruelest wrongs. He who, in any measure, and by any method, whether it be the mother with her child at her knee, or the teacher face to face with his class, or the lecturer, or the author, or the preacher, is establishing men in the faith of God, and quickening their sense of dependence on God, and making them feel more and more the obligations they are under to obey the commands of God, is aiding individuals not only to realize the highest type of excellence known to the world, but is brightening the prospect for all humanity. It is not merely piety which is subserved, it is good morals as well, when men can be induced to look up and say, lovingly and sincerely and with the whole soul: *Our Father who art in heaven.*

MYSTERY IN THE NEW BIRTH.

How can these things be? John 3: 9.

NICODEMUS was perplexed by the teaching of our Lord concerning the regeneration of the soul. Others since his day have experienced the same difficulty, and the question asked by this "man of the Pharisees" has often been on the lips of earnest searchers after the truth. It seems a fit thing, therefore, to follow along on the line of the interrogation here submitted, and devote the time we are able to spend together to a consideration of the subject of *Mystery in the New Birth.*

This ruler of the Jews who had come to Jesus by night is not to be blamed for his desire to obtain a better understanding of what had been told him. In all healthy souls the desire to know is instinctive. Nature provokes questions. Men ask questions. The disposition is general to get at facts, and the causes and secrets of facts.

The father who, in his impatience, petulantly exclaims to his inquisitive child: "I do wish you wouldn't ask so many questions — ", often giving a peculiar sting to the remark by calling them "*foolish questions,*" is not only recreant to his sacred duties as a parent, but he is at war with the divine arrangement. It is a necessity of its nature, — God has made it so — that every intelligent child should be a persistent questioner.

Further along in life this investigating impulse is of incalculable value. It is the spring of progress. Out of it come discoveries, inventions, explorations, developments in art and science, forward movements in politics and law and the institutions of society. It is a fruitful and beneficent impulse. Inspiration recognizes and appeals to it. The language of the Word is "*Search.*" If there be those, as we are sometimes told there are, who still take the ground that there is no call to think, or that for any reason it is perilous to think, it is very clear they have no warrant for their position in the Bible. "What think ye?" is a challenge which fell from our Lord's own lips.

This questioning can be carried too far. It can be carried beyond reasonable and helpful limits. In dealing with religious problems it often is. Instead of following the desire to know straight on to its proper conclusion, and there resting, as in other departments of investigation, men often give way to the desire, and keep on asking and asking, till they slide off into the spirit of over-curiousness which turns a thing end for end, and in and out, and weighs and gauges and tests, and yet is never satisfied. This is not studying, it is torturing truth. It is not investigating, it is crucifying truth. To deal so with truth is to distrust and dishonor truth.

Men do not get on in this way, either. An end-less scrutiny imparts no headway. Under this pro-cess people are quite likely to become more and more uncertain, and very sure to grow dry and shriveled of soul.

While, as has already been said, Nicodemus is not to be blamed for his desire to come into a bet-ter understanding of what had been told him, still his question has in it just a little of this over-inquisi-tive tone. It is a push out into the realm of the un-explored and baffling. Christ had said to him that he must be born anew, or born from above. To give him an idea of the way the Spirit works in renewing the soul, He had brought forward the analogy of the wind. Men feel the force of the wind; they see the effect of it; but whence it cometh and whither it go-eth are things hidden. So is the new birth. But this was not enough. Nicodemus wanted all doubt removed, and all perplexities involved in the change untwisted and straightened out. Everything must be clear and intelligible in the path along which his feet were to tread, or he would not move forward at all. The underlying thought with him seems to have been that mystery bars advance; and that in-ability to understand fully the mode in which God in-fluences a soul in renewing its spiritual life is a valid reason, or a reason at any rate over which one may long hesitate, for not accepting the fact of such influ-ence. But this attitude, taken by him whom our Lord called "the teacher of Israel," and held still by not a few reflecting people, cannot be maintained.

I. *For, to begin with, we cannot fully understand anything*.

If this is to be the ground on which we will consent to recognize a fact or a truth — that we know it all through and through — we can recognize nothing. Or to put it the other way, if we feel bound to oppose everything which we do not know through and through, know in all its causes and relations and methods — then life for most from start to end will be an open and pronounced dissent, and we shall be saying "no," "no," to every reality in the universe.

1. *Take, first of all, what seems to be widest removed from any possible question — the simple fact of the existence of things*.

We do not any of us hesitate to be very positive in the opinion that things do exist. We look abroad and we say the earth *is*. We look up and we say the sun *is*. Trees, brooks, forests, oceans, mountains — these *are*. Speculative philosophy has called in question the existence of matter. Common sense never does. Common sense has the utmost confidence that stars and continents and bodies are realities. But when the attempt is made to strike through and get at the further fact of the how of it all, men are brought to pause. There are any number of theories as to the origin of matter. Some say it is self-existent. Over any given form of matter some have at hand the word "evolution." Some go behind all this and utter the word — *God*. This is the solution most of us accept. God *created* the heavens and the earth.

This is the *why* of it.   The question of *how* is still
unanswered.   How did things which were not come
to be?   Who has the faculty to tell us, or the faculty
to comprehend it?   Here things are.   To dispute
these open palpable facts is a sign, if not of downright insanity, yet of philosophical madness.   Not
to act on the basis of these facts is criminal folly.
But the simple matter of the *mode* in which things
existing have come to exist — how about this?   Who
will give us light?

2.   *From the fact of simple existence advance to
the fact of organic existence.*

The forester plants an acorn; it swells into an
oak.   How?   How is it that the mere bit of matter
which a child can hold between thumb and finger
manages to rise into the magnificent proportions of
the solid tree?   How does it start?   How does it
know when to start?   What makes it think of start-
ing?   How from earth and air and water and sunshine does it contrive to absorb the materials of
growth, and the strength to hold steady front against
storm and tempest?   How has so much dead matter
in the soil become so much living force in the oak?
How have all these tons of timber in trunk and branch
got themselves lifted up there so high in air?   How
is this cunning process of distribution carried on,
and so successfully that stem and limb and leaf and
bud and fruit receive each the supplies fitted to nour-
ish them?   We say, we have to say, God gives the
life-germ of the tree;   He furnishes the elements of

development; and He determines the laws of development. But all this is the cause of what we see. The
question now up is the question of *how*. How can
a plant grow? How can matter with only an acorn
to start from ever get up into a majestic oak? Perhaps there is somebody who can tell us. If so, he
may be assured the world wants to hear him.

3. *Move forward still another step into the
sphere of the rational and moral.*

How manifold the wonders! How elusive the
secrets!

Here is the *will*. Everybody is familiar with the
control exercised by the will over the bodily organs,
and how these organs are used as instruments of the
will. By simple volition a man lifts his hand, holds
it suspended, moves it back and forth, and lets it fall
again. By simple volition energy is infused into
the hand to hold the plow, to shove the plane, to
guide the helm, to use the pen, and to strike, if need
be, sturdy blows for country. But what is this mysterious power? Where does it reside? How does
it come into this communication with physical organs? We look wise and say the nerves are the
sensitive wires along which these messages are trans-
mitted from brain to finger-tip. Yes. But what are
the nerves? What makes the nerves so sensitive and
responsive? How does this strange sovereignty of a
thought or wish or purpose, come into such instant
ascendency over the whole commonwealth of the
body? There is never a voluntary movement with-

out this operation of the will upon the organs of motion.   How is it all?   Who will explain to us the
mysteries of it?

Here is the *memory*.   This man is three score and
ten.   These sixty or seventy years have taken him
through many changing scenes and events.   He sits
to-day with whitened locks, thinking it will not be
long before he is gathered to his fathers.   His
thoughts run forward to the rest that remaineth, and
to the new scenes which will break on his vision out
beyond these earthly horizons.   But as he is able to
look forward in anticipation, so also may he turn his
gaze backward.   By a simple, easy transition he
covers all the spaces of the intervening years, and
takes his place amidst the associations and surround-
ings of his childhood.   The sacred incidents of the
past rush in upon him, and he stands once more in
the hallowed circle of the old sweet home.   He
grasps the "vanished hand" of a father.   He gives
back a sainted mother's kiss.   He fills his wonted
place at the table.   He is one of a happy group who
gather about the hearth-stone, where he listens
again to the old familiar stories.   He roams the fields
and the woods, and mingles in all the favorite sports
of the long-gone years.   He hears the voices, sees
the faces, and recalls the characteristic expressions
of friends many years dead.   The garden, the brook,
the well, the orchard, the hills,—they are all there,
fresh in the mind once more.   The pulse beats
quicker; the eyes flash with a new brightness; old

associations revive, and the laughing and the weeping, the old perplexities and the triumphs of the early days, become almost fresh experiences of the life.

It makes no difference where this old home may have been. Back amidst the mountains, the apple-trees, the forests and streams, the sweet little hamlets and villages of dear New England; or across the seas amidst the lawns and hedgerows and hollies and ancient mounds and grand cathedrals of Old England; or away in rugged Scotland; or in France or Italy warm with a sunshine which needs only to be caught and fixed to become song and picture, it is all the same. Memory is the magician whose waving wand takes us instantly back to the sacred spot of our childhood and youth.

Again how is it? There is no doubt about the fact of what memory can do. But how? How is it that this man of seventy years can take hold of the silken thread of what we call memory, and find his way back through the alleys and chambers of the labyrinth of his vanished hours, till he stands again in the presence of the old scenes and associates, and locks hands with men and women and little children who have long since gone to their final reward? The function of what goes by the name of memory; ways of strengthening the memory; the pleasures and pains associated with the process of recalling our yesterdays, we know well enough. In other words, when we ask what memory is, and what its uses are, and how to make it more serviceable, the answer is forthcoming. But when we ask — How? How can all this be done? nobody volunteers to give information.

The same is true of all mental operations. Questions can be asked concerning every act of the mind which no man can answer. Mysteries are everywhere. The realm of nature is full of them. The realm of thought is full of them.

Hence the man who lays down the principle that he will not act until he fully understands everything entering into his action, will never act at all. The act by which a man becomes a child of God in a new and distinct sense through the inbreathing of the Divine Spirit is not singular in that it involves mysteries; this it shares in common with all nature. Consequently he who rejects the new birth on the ground that there are mysteries in it — just as our Lord said there are — must reject everything. He must reject the fact of his own existence; of all existence; of growth and all such facts as are brought to light in any kind of intellectual activity. He must act as no sane man ever does act, save in the sphere of his religious obligations and privileges.

II.   *In the second place, while we cannot fully understand anything, and the mode in which God influences the soul in regeneration is involved in mystery, the fact that such influence is exerted and that under this influence life is changed and made new is beyond question.*

If there is anything in human experience, or human history, which is true, it is true that the hearts of men are sometimes wrought upon and wholly reversed in the spirit and current and hope of them by the grace of God.

1. *This is made evident in altered character.*

There are transformations of character so sudden, radical and permanent, that we are sure they must have been brought about by supernatural influence. The transformation is so marked that it calls for the power of God. It is so beneficent that it can be explained only by the goodness of God.

If it be not a matter of experience with any of us, it is yet a matter of observation that such changes do take place. We have seen voluptuousness changed into chastity. We have seen debauchery changed into temperance. We have seen irritability grow patient. We have seen wasting prodigality become careful economy. We have seen stinginess and greed give way to a sweet habit of benevolence. We have seen men who are profane and reckless fall under deep and quick conviction and take their places in the ranks of the devout. We have seen morose and savage tempers toned down into childlike softness. We have seen vice expelled from hearts where it was long regnant, and virtue enthroned. We have seen men who were proud and lawless and profligate, men who cared nothing for divine command, and mocked at all holy things, turned about and transformed into genuine and whole-souled children of God.

Take an instance like that of John Newton. Born in London, the only child of his mother, who died when her boy was but seven years of age; a sailor at eleven; impressed and taken on board a warship at seventeen; a deserter, without any faith in God and with all moral restraint thrown off, caught, brought back, degraded to the lowest position and flogged and ironed, at twenty; in the service of a slave-dealer on the African coast, and lost apparently to everything save a sense of his own wretchedness, at twenty-three; a slave-trader, carrying hundreds of poor Negroes from their native land to the West Indies, before he was thirty; yet through the grace of God in Christ this man was made a new creature, and through the same grace of God in Christ one of the most earnest and useful servants of the Lord in his day and generation. His epitaph, written by himself, tells the story of the radical transformation he experienced: "John Newton, Clerk, once an Infidel and Libertine, a servant of slaves in Africa, was, by the rich mercy of our Lord and Saviour, Jesus Christ, preserved, restored, pardoned, and appointed to preach the faith he had long labored to destroy." It was not by a process of reformation merely; it was by a process of regeneration that the character of Newton was transformed. He was born again, — born from above; and nothing else will account for the change experienced by him and witnessed in him.

Take the instance of Paul. Look at this man be-

fore and after the journey to Damascus. Compare
the two in their dispositions and purposes. One of
them is breathing out threatening and slaughter; the
other is breathing out supplication and thanksgiving
and praise. One of them is exceeding mad against
the disciples of our Lord; the other joyfully sub-
scribes himself the "servant" of the Lord. In their
feelings, in their aims, and in their actions, the two
men are as wide apart as the poles. The change
was complete. It was sudden. It was not a growth.
It was not a process with stages. It was an out-and-
out transformation. It was a revolution in all the
thoughts and plans and sympathies and intentions of
the man. It was as instantaneous as a blow. It
was as effective as a fiat of God.

It is no use to say the men in whom these transformations seem to have been wrought, were deceived
in what had occurred, — they were not. It is no use
to say, we who make a study of their cases are deceived; we are not. These souls came under a Power
not ourselves, which makes for righteousness, and
they knew it. They knew they had been breathed
upon by a breath out of heaven, and were changed
by it. Newton was not deluded. Neither was
Paul. Nor was John Wesley, nor Martin Luther,
nor Jonathan Edwards, nor Pascal, nor Madame
Guyon, nor Payson, nor Horace Bushnell, nor Ly-
man Beecher, nor Nettleton, nor Finney, nor Phillips Brooks, nor Spurgeon. Hearts do come under
the influence of God; and they are purified and ex-

alted and brought into new relations by these influences. To this fact millions of souls are glad witnesses.

2.   *The fact is made still further evident by what men succeed in doing.*

Men do what they neither would do nor could do, were they not under an influence from God, and helped and sustained by the grace of what He is able to do.

In consequence of the massacre of St. Bartholomew, on that August night in 1572, when not less than 35,000 souls were treacherously slaughtered, and the dreadful persecution to which Protestants in France were subjected in after years, the Huguenots were forced to flee into all sorts of places for refuge. They were only too happy if they could secure shelter anywhere from the fierce storms of wrath which burst upon them. A little company of these somehow found their way up into a natural fastness called Steinthal, a wild district in the Vosges Mountains. Here they lived for a hundred and fifty years or more in poverty and hardships and isolation. They were not in the live current of the world's thought and progress, and they knew nothing of the movements of civilization. Hence, as would naturally be expected, it fared ill with them.

The teachers and preachers who came with them into this secluded and sterile spot, and their immediate successors had long been dead. Gradually it came to pass that they had no teachers and preachers.

Schools worthy of the name, churches, family altars, the influence of religious sentiment and life, were all gone. In their place were ignorance, stolidity, and a degradation which was not only pitiable but repulsive. The people lived in cabins and huts. There was nothing which might be called a road in the whole district. In the short summers they gathered a little food. In the long winters they often herded with the cattle in the stables for warmth. Outside of wild barbaric tribes it would have been hard to find a match to the material and moral degradation of this degenerate colony of French Huguenots.

On August 31, in the year of our Lord 1740, at Strasburg, in Alsatia, there was born a child whose destiny, in the providence of God, was to be closely interwoven with the destiny of the wretched community just described, and whose name was to become one of the inspiring and cherished names of history. The child grew into a lad. Under wholesome home training, the lad became an earnest, scholarly boy. At fifteen he entered the University at Strasburg. At eighteen he was a Bachelor of Arts. At twenty he had been ordained to the gospel ministry, with a view to service in the Lutheran church. At twenty-seven, though, as has been said, he had taken upon himself the ordination vows of the ministry, he was still in his study. It was his idea, evidently, that for large usefulness there must be faithful and patient preparation.

At this period in his career a humble missionary,

who confessed his own inability to gain access to them, stood before him, and told the story of these wild and degraded mountaineers. On the basis of his story he made an appeal. He wanted this devoted student to go to this people and be their shepherd. He wanted him to take his magnificent mental endowments, his social position, his wide learning, his culture, his hopes of promotion, and lay them all on the altar of a community whose one bond of sympathy between him and them was that they were both human. He was fitted for a Professor's Chair in the University he so much loved. He had the talents and the training to justify him in anticipating advancement to almost any place open to the men of his time. He was asked to subordinate it all, nay, to consecrate it all to the welfare of these rude men and women in the well-nigh inaccessible region of Steinthal. Could much more be asked?

After a deep and earnest struggle, in which it was made clear to his own soul that the call which had reached him was the call of God, he said yes and went. He became their spiritual guide and teacher and friend. It was like the breaking in on them of a new sun in the heavens. It was like the changing of their long, cold winters into tropic warmth. It was like the broadening out of their horizons till they saw the resplendent beauty and felt the pulse of the great world about them. Into the low and sluggish life of this pitiable people he poured the hot and stimulating blood of his own choice life. The place was desolate and solitary; he made it glad.   It was a wilderness; at his touch it blossomed like a rose.

For fifty-nine years, or until he was eighty-six years of age, this devoted servant of Jesus Christ had his home amongst these people, away in this wild and remote district.   He prayed for them; he taught them; he preached to them; he bore their burdens; he toiled with his own hands at the hardest tasks, that they might the better know how to toil, and be the more willing to toil; he carried them in his thought and heart, as only one can who has caught the vicarious spirit of Jesus; and then, abundantly ready for his home-going, he heard and answered another call of God, and went up to dwell in the heights of the New Jerusalem.

It was a marvelous record the man made.   The vulgar, the despised community to whom he was introduced a little less than three score years before his final retirement from them, had been made over new, and the dominion of coarseness and vice into whose subjection they had come, had given way to a dominion of gentle manners and good morals. Many had come into a personal experience of the saving grace of God in Christ.   There were Christian churches, Christian homes, Christian schools. There were other institutions designed to be helpful in a Christian way.   There was a Christian public sentiment.   The community had risen to the point where it had pride in itself, — self-respect and aspirations.   One saw everywhere the evidences of thrift and comfort. Moreover this work was done in such wise and thorough fashion that it abides. Seventy years after the death of this servant of God the fountains he opened are still flowing.

But who was this large soul? this lad of brilliant promise? this successful student? this man of stalwart strength, and heroic purpose, and fine culture? this devoted and beloved pastor? this exponent of human brotherhood? this brave philanthropist, and uncompromising advocate of the rights of all to to a fair chance in life? Very fitly may the name be spoken in tones of love and reverence, for it was — *John Frederick Oberlin*.

Now how account for a life and a service like this? Can it be done on any other theory than that the man was transformed, and made what he was, by the renewing grace of God in Christ? If we look at him from the point of his talents, and what he might have done with them, or from the point of his labors, the amount of them, the place and condition of them, and the temper in which they were conducted, can we escape the inference that his soul must have been touched and quickened by divine influence? Can we get away from the conclusion that he must have had experience of God, and did his work guided by the power of God?

What other adequate motive can be conjectured? *Ease?* There was no ease in his life. *Wealth?* One smiles at the suggestion. *Fame?* Not thus do men seek fame. The man secured fame, but he did not know he was going to do it.

Thus we have a whole line of facts, — these radical changes wrought in character, and the spirit of consecration to hard and disagreeable tasks, of which the instance given is but one out of multitudes, which can be explained on no other supposition than that men are born anew. Be the difficulties involved in the fact what they may, and a proper philosophy of the fact never so hard to formulate, here the fact is; and it is a fact altogether too evident and robust to be set aside by anybody's denial of it. Men are renewed and empowered by the grace of God in Christ.

III. *But, in the third place, while conceding an element of profound mystery in the process of the new birth, there is yet no valid reason for not accepting the fact of the new birth, because the fact admits of explanations and illustrations which would be deemed satisfactory with reference to other subjects of investigation.*

To all minds not utterly given over to atheism it ought to be a sufficient explanation just to say: *God does it.* This is what Jesus says: "Born of the Spirit." This is what the Apostle says: "For it is God that worketh in you." To this point we are forced at last with all our mysteries. This is the ultimate solution of everything, — the only real solution of anything: God does it.

The bird sits and sings because God has tuned its throat to harmony, and put into its heart the impulse of song. The bud expands under the in-

fluence of sunshine and shower, and unfolds into
all the richness and beauty of the full-blown rose,
in exact accord with a law God has put into its
germ. The chemist in his laboratory gets back
to a point where he is obliged to go behind "nature" and say — *God.* The geologist, after all his
searchings and wanderings, must come round and
stand with bowed head and awed spirit in presence of the sublime sentence: "In the beginning —
God." To Him as the Cause of causes, and the
Philosophy of philosophies, all things struggle up.
Toward this conclusion science itself is now moving.
It is found impossible to get on without the final fact
of God.

Hence the bringing of a life under the power of
the Spirit, and renewing it in the divine image, rests
not merely on like, but on the identical ground on
which, sooner or later, we are obliged to place everything. The renewing of the soul is a divine work.
It is wrought by divine energy, and after a divine
manner. As we live naturally because He breathes
into us the breath of a natural life, so we live spiritually because He breathes into us the breath of a
spiritual life.

But Christ did not pause with this simple reference
of the new birth to God. On first view He seems not
to have made, or attempted to make, any explanation
beyond the bare assertion that whatever change may
be wrought is to be referred directly to God. Still
He does go further; and what He says further is
aflame with light.

It is a curious and instructive fact that the word which is here translated "Spirit" is the same word which is translated "wind" or "air." Air, the most pervasive and subtle of the common elements, is made the special symbol of the Spirit. It is chosen as the vehicle for conveying a true idea of the invisible and mysterious nature of the Spirit. It looks as though Christ meant to say something like this: The Spirit of God, like the air we breathe, is evermore about us, filling all things, penetrating all things, sustaining all things, and is the element in which the soul lives.

We are not always conscious of the presence of the Spirit. We judge of Him as we do of the wind — by the effects. We sit at our window on a calm, still day, and look out upon the trees. They are motionless. There is no rocking of leaf-crowned tops; no bending of stout old trunks. Every branch seems asleep on the bosom of the atmosphere. Suddenly the leaves begin to quiver, and faint murmurs steal in from the green recesses. The slumbering boughs awake from their repose; the elastic limbs leap in ecstasy of life; huge stems whose strength has been compacted from the centuries bow under the pressure; the neighboring boughs smite each other, and the whole forest sways and surges before the majesty of the on-sweeping wind. For the winds are abroad. Whence they come, or whither they go, we know not; but here they are. We feel their presence. We see their power.

This is the way it may be with the Spirit of God.
Ordinarily the Spirit may not press Himself on
our attention. We repose in Him so softly; His
solicitations are so delicate, we are not conscious
of His presence. By and by there comes a Pentecostal outpouring, a great awakening which pervades
the whole land, and makes an epoch in religious
history, — and then we say: "The Spirit is abroad."
We witness the tokens of Him everywhere. He
is swaying the hearts of men as tempests bend
the forests. Persons proud with earthly gains and
prospects He smites down. He dashes prejudice
in pieces, as the wind dashes down decayed trunks.
He uproots what is old and ready to perish, and sifts
in with a stern husbandry the seeds of the new. He
is a breath right out of the heavens from God; and
He clarifies and renews the souls which recognize
Him, and yield to His power.

So far, therefore, as natural things can be made to
represent the things of the Spirit, the air, sometimes
at rest, sometimes in motion, at all times encompassing
the earth, and pervading and filling every possible
recess, may be taken as the symbol of the ever-
active, all-pervasive and renewing Energy which we
call the Holy Ghost. With our bodily eyes we do
not see these movements; but we feel them, and
know them to be realities by the power that is in
them.

It remains to suggest, or rather to entreat, that we
straightway act in this great concern of the soul as

we do in all the lesser matters of life. We do not refuse to think until we are masters of all the intricate laws of thought. We do not refuse to put forth volitions until we understand all the secrets of the will. On the contrary we let mind and will work freely, and we place confidence in their working. We do not shut ourselves up in dark rooms, and exclude the light, because we do not perfectly comprehend all the problems and laws of light; we live in it and rejoice in it. This is what we do in the whole circle of our every-day life. We act on the fact of our own existence. We act on the fact of our possession of certain capabilities, physical, mental, moral. We act on the fact of a definite relationship to our environment, even though there be thousands upon thousands of secrets in all these things which we have never studied out, and, while we remain in the body at any rate, never shall study out. Why not act on the fact of God, and the fact of the soul, and the fact that through faith in Christ, and the ministry of the Divine Spirit, God and the soul, which is now separated from God by sin and alienation, may be brought together?

How much better, here and now, to cast aside all the sophistries and quibblings concerning the method of the birth from above, and respond heartily to the invitations our Divine Lord lovingly addresses to all who are strangers to the promises, and without any sure foundation to the hope of eternal life, to come into the fellowship of God, and walk in the joy of a new creation in Christ while yet on earth, that when the scenes of life on earth are over, there may be a walking in the joy of a new creation in Christ through the endless ages!

SPIRITUAL CAPITAL.

For whosoever hath, to him shall be given, and he shall have abundance; but whosoever hath not, from him shall be taken away even that which he hath. Matt. 13: 12.

FOLLOWING out the thought these words suggest, we shall be led to consider the subject of *Spiritual Capital.* This consideration, however, will be with special reference to the way in which such capital may be increased and how diminished and wasted.

Already an accepted maxim, probably, Jesus took these words up and recast them and set to them the seal of His own name and made them current coin forever.

In substance, we find this passage five times in the New Testament; but the lessons sought to be drawn from it are only two.

In connection with the Parable of the Sower, these words are used to emphasize the responsibility of the soul in receiving the Word of God and nurturing it into fruitfulness. In connection with the Parable of the Talents they are brought forward to impress the duty of developing the faculties and improving to the utmost the opportunities which may have been given to one by the Divine Father. The text, therefore, is a sort of mirror, which reflects the image of

whatever falls upon it.   On the one hand, it gathers
up and throws back in clear, sharp outline, the issues
which wait upon fidelity.   On the other hand, it discloses the awful consequences which must follow
disregard of duty, whether in the sphere of hearing
or doing.

It is very much as though the Great Teacher had
said: "To receive sincerely every truth which may
be communicated — this is the only safeguard against
disastrous and utter loss, not only of the truth one
already has, but of the receiving capacity;" and:
"To do promptly every known duty, and to discharge
faithfully every trust committed — this is the only
condition on which advance in knowledge and in
character can be secured."

To put it in still another way.   To have and to
use well what one has is to make sure of increase in
possessions.   To have and to use ill, or to use as
though one had not and did not care to have, is to
make sure of decrease in possessions.

In illustration of this it may be observed that:

I.   *The practical on-goings of our every-day life
prepare us to anticipate the existence and operation of some such law in the higher realm of the
moral and spiritual nature.*

Precisely this, indeed, is what is all the time taking place within the circle of our own experience and
observation.   "To him that hath is given; from him
that hath not is taken away, even that which he
hath."

In business spheres the law may be said to be well-nigh, if not absolutely, universal. Naturally enough; for it was in business spheres that our Lord found this maxim. It grew out of financial transactions. In the mint of the exchanges and the markets it had its original coining. Shop-keepers, buyers and sellers made it into a proverb. Whoever else might deny them, men in commercial life had to accept these words as they fell from the lips of Jesus, because they embodied a truth to which trade itself, in both its successes and failures, had given currency.

Men saw, for instance, that if one was rich and cared to be richer, he could easily become so. They saw that if one was poor, and did not struggle wisely and resolutely against poverty, he would become poorer and poorer.

They see the same thing still. The law works now as of old. Wealth attracts wealth. One house grows readily into two houses, and then into four and a dozen. Shekels invested with foresight speedily reproduce other shekels. Large estates, by a little shrewd manœuvring, are made to swallow up all the lesser estates about them; while those who are dependent, either through natural incompetency, or through inability to embrace opportunities which chance to open to them, or the steady accumulation of their indebtedness, which is quite sure to result in the crumbling away of all their possessions, become more and more dependent till the solemn hour when rich and poor alike lie down in the grave, and all

material distinctions are blotted out forever. There
is nothing exceptional in this fact. Across in Jerusalem, here in Chicago, back in the old times of two
thousand years ago and amidst the bustling activity
of these latest times, property in a cunning man's
hands is a magnet sure to draw other properties to
itself. A dollar in possession of one who knows
how to use it thriftily straightway becomes a net
with which to catch other dollars. Pounds, shillings
and pence have a kind of gregarious or social quality
in them — they like to be together. Does anybody
know of anything which seems quite so lonesome as
the last dime in one's pocket? It wants to get out
and away where it can have company. There is a
sort of mutual attractiveness in these shining bits of
silver and gold, and it is hard to keep the few from
joining the many.

It is amongst the cardinal laws of accumulation
that the way to get much is first to get little. The
way to lose all, and to block the paths that lead to
any bettering of condition, is to be improvident and
careless about what one has already. It is over the
small beginnings of a fortune that the struggle is always sharpest. To start is the difficulty. The first
thousand is the hard thousand to win. John Jacob
Astor, in his old age, is reported to have said: Given
these two alternatives, to start from where he started
with nothing and work his way into possession of ten
hundred dollars, or to go on from the ten hundred
and amass the large amount he gathered together,

he would accept the latter alternative. Ordinarily it would be easier. In buying and selling, large, strong firms are masters of the situation. They can take advantage of all the fluctuations in the market. They can trim their ships so as to make every wind a favoring gale. It is said that at fifty Peabody was worth only fifty thousand dollars. But with that sum in hand, coupled with the skill and care which had enabled him to climb up from poverty to that round of the ladder, he could harvest wealth almost as he would. From that moment events became his servants, and wars and revolutions and national disasters and embarrassments could be forced to pay tribute to his treasury. Saying nothing now about the morality of their schemes and methods, what a simple matter it was, after they once got going, for the Vanderbilts and Goulds to make their millions! To possess largely is to hold the key with which one can unlock the door and range at will through all most promising possibilities. But want is a withe with which the hands are tied, so that one cannot reach forth and pluck the boughs, even though he stands in the midst of them and sees that they are all laden with rare and ripened fruit.

Take it in the line of the successive generations, and Pharaoh's dream is quite likely to have ample illustration. The sons of the rich, through overmuch indulgence and pampering, are liable to lack the industry and economy and foresight in caring for it, which were shown in the accumulation of the inheritance that has descended to them. But take it in any given generation where men stand side by side, and it is the "fat kine" which will eat up "the lean and ill-favored kine;" and it is the "good ears" which will "devour the thin ears."

Advantage is often taken of this law to work great harm. Huge monopolies are built up, trusts are formed. The strong combine against the weak and crush them. Justice is overridden and equity is outraged. Proper remedies must be invoked. But the law, like a thousand other laws of which advantage is taken, still exists. If a man has no capacity to accumulate, or does not care to accumulate, or wishing to accumulate is yet crippled in resources and opportunities, he can make little or no headway. If he possesses already he can easily add to his possessions. To him that hath shall be given. From him that hath not shall be taken.

II. *In the higher sphere of the mental and æsthetic nature there are facts prophetic of this same law which Christ announced as dominant in the spiritual world.*

Indeed, as we rise in the scale, the law becomes more and more obvious. Seen in business realms, it is seen still more clearly in the realms of knowledge and beauty. For in pure brain-quests there is less room for the play of accident than in markets and exchanges, and one can get absolutely nothing which he is not in some measure fitted to receive.

Here, for instance, are two men side by side. One

of them can read and the other can not. As touching the whole mass of information which is in books, what a difference there is in their possibilities! One can make historians instruct him, and philosophers guide and quicken him, and poets delight him, and essayists stir his soul to a high enthusiasm. The other, though he stand in the midst of all libraries — the Bodleian at Oxford, the British Museum in London, the National at Paris, or the Imperial at St. Petersburg, — can get nothing out of them. These millions of books are but so many cords of blotted paper, bound up in so many pounds or square yards of sheep-skin or calf. One can make the centuries bring their garnered wealth and lay it down at his feet. The other can know the story of the past only as he picks it up through oral traditions or sees it in the institutions and life before him. Wanting in the simple capacity to read, he is wanting in the capacity which will enable him to make good his title to the rare and vast treasures which printed volumes contain. A little knowledge opens the way to more knowledge; but nothing yields nothing.

Men sometimes marvel at the number of languages certain scholars have been able to master. Elihu Burritt, the "Learned Blacksmith," for instance, is said to have had a knowledge of "Latin, Greek, Hebrew, Arabic and other Oriental tongues, and almost all modern European and Slavonic languages." It is partly marvelous and partly not. Of course it all argues special linguistic capacity. Some men in virtue of natural aptitude for this kind of learning can get along much faster and go much further than others. But all languages have a certain affinity. Within certain classes the relationship is very close. Hence when the student has acquired one language the second comes easier. Two tongues thoroughly conquered make the third one yield still more readily. So on. The more wide and varied a man's knowledge of the languages of the earth, the greater will be the facility with which he will overcome the difficulties of new speech. To him that hath.

Surprise, too, is often expressed at the amount of information which can be brought together and stored away in the mind of a single individual. The younger Alexander of Princeton, Lord Macaulay, and Mr. Gladstone might be cited as examples. These names stand for walking encyclopædias. But that they came to know so much is not wholly surprising. Accumulations like these imply an ability far above the average, it is true, and great diligence in research and remarkable classifying power and retentive memories. Yet facts, like languages, have a sort of co-ordinating thread running through them. One fact thoroughly known opens the door to an easy acquaintance with a second, and these two to still a third, and so on indefinitely. He who studies history wisely is like a recruiting officer who makes each newly enlisted man an agent to bring in others. The more the ranks swell the more they are likely to swell. Let one become acquainted with a particu-

lar era, as the era of the Egyptian Pharaohs, the
Jewish monarchy, the Grecian philosophy, the Augustine age of Rome, or the age of Constantine, or
Charlemagne, or Elizabeth, or Washington, and he
can compass some closely related second period
much quicker. Let one become familiar with the
career of some single nation — England, say, or
France, or Spain, or Italy, or Germany, or Russia,
or the United States, and one by one the unexplored
annals of the other nations will come forward to
open up their secrets. For each touches the other
at so many points, literature, diplomacy, invention,
dynastic intercourse, wars and revolutions, that in
learning of one much has already been learned of the
others. As the study-point shifts the seeing will be
of different sides of facts; but the facts will be substantially the same.

It is the same in the domain of the arts and sciences.
It is to the instructed mind, the trained eye and ear,
that the heavens and the earth teem with communications. One knowing no astronomy stands out of
an evening under the deep vault of the overarching
sky, and sees countless orbs flashing like gems
out of far-away depths. A certain impression of
beauty, majesty, power, wisdom, and of sweet divine
beneficence is made on him, and that is all. To an
astronomer, who knows all these burning worlds by
name, who knows their orbits, their revolutions, their
dimensions, their influence one upon another, there
comes this same impression, and how much more!

One knowing nothing of botany wanders through the fields and beholds the flowers, and they minister to him a measure of pleasure. But how much that is subtle and delicate and exquisite in their forms and modes of development there is, which can be appreciated only by a person who is up in the lore of flowers! To an intelligent and enthusiastic botanist the flowers are gracious, confidential; and they tell him secrets they never so much as hint to other people. Professor Dana climbs the mountains and roams through the valleys; he rides in and out of the deep cuts along the railroad lines; his quick eye sees the likenesses and unlikenesses in composition of soils and rocks, and everything, everywhere he goes, has a wonderful story to tell him. The rocks are more than rocks as he looks upon them; they are open volumes wherein there are thoughts written by the finger of God. Layers upon layers in the structure of the globe are well-preserved annals of the long-gone ages. These facts are not disclosed to everybody. For nature is fastidious. She will yield her secrets to trained minds, but not to those ignorant of their significance.

We, all of us, catch this trick of nature, and act in the same way. Let a man become distinguished as an antiquarian, and how all the world will rush to him with relics! Let it be known that a lawyer is crowded with cases, or that a physician is overrun with patients, and what a multitude will flock to him for counsel or treatment! Pack a church and everybody will want to get into it. When scholars pass from country to country it is scholars they go to see. Eminence in art, or science, or literature, attracts to itself corresponding eminence. It was to Gough, who already had so many he did not know what to do with them, that men told their charming stories, or their harrowing tales of domestic life and of the ruin and rescue of homes. Having much of this kind of information, men hurried to him with more. It was to Garrison and Smith and Beecher and Lovejoy and Jocelyn and Mrs. Stowe that men used to run with accounts of slaves, — their trials, their escapes, their plans and feelings and hopes, and so added to stores of knowledge which were already large. It was to Audubon, whose acquaintance with birds was so intimate and ample, and not to those who knew nothing about birds, that everybody rushed with fresh discoveries of the haunts and habits of birds. It was to Agassiz, whose cabinet was stored with wonders, that every strange specimen of fish and shell and reptile was straightway expressed. When Professor Felton was alive, and stood at the head of Greek scholars in America, and later when Professor Hadley succeeded to this place, all other Greek scholars were ready to lay their treasures of research at his feet. It is to those who have abundant supplies of books that books are most likely to be given by authors and publishers.

Evidently — so evidently that nobody can fail to see it — it is not need which regulates in these matters.

The needs are all the other way. It is those who are supplied to fullness who are supplied still more. It is those who lack who are left lacking still. Men carry their contributions of fact as they do their sacks of grain, to the mills where they feel sure they can be ground. A garment cannot be hung up if there is no pin to hang it on. There can be no giving where there is no capacity to receive. Music, poetry, fine sentiment, and all the finer expressions of the soul, are thrown away upon one who is without an open eye and an open ear and an aptitude to take in these forms of thought and feeling. All through the realm of mind, and all through the realm of taste, it is and it must be to him that hath.

III. *Advancing now to the position to which all these facts have been pointing, it may be said that in spiritual spheres the law announced by our Lord is absolute.*

In force in a general way in the accumulation of property, and in force still more rigidly in matters of knowledge and taste, in the range of those higher faculties with which God is apprehended and approaches to God are made, and which come into play in the living of a godly life on earth, there may be said to be no exception to the law.

This will appear from a few specifications.

1. *It is to souls which have in them some measure of faith, and use it, that larger measures of faith are given.*

It is not merely true that faith is rewarded, and

that disclosures richer and more abundant are made to faith as it is exercised, but the faith itself grows and becomes stronger and stronger as it is put under the strain of a wise and healthy activity. The man who believes in God, and moves forward under inspiration of this belief, comes in no long time to believe in God more easily and fully, and to put a more unquestioning trust in all His promises and providences.

This is brought out in the story of Abraham. He appeared on the stage as a man of faith. God spoke to him. He believed. Because he believed he obeyed. He put what faith he had into practice, and made it his working capital. But is it not clear that his faith grew through use, and was equal to harder tasks at the end of his career than at the beginning? When word came to him there in Mesopotamia, before, as Stephen tells us, he dwelt in Haran, directing him to leave native land and kindred and enter a land which was to be shown him, but of which as yet he knew nothing, he was subjected to a severe test, and it is to his everlasting glory that he was equal to it; but there was nothing in this to go to the heart-strings, and stagger the soul by working confusion in past dealings and future prospects, as under the order, through which "God did prove Abraham," to take his son, his one son, whom he loved, even Isaac, and journey away with him to the land of Moriah. He exercised faith in God, and by exercise developed his faith, until it was equal to this tremendous strain.

God can be a living Presence to the soul only when the soul has an eye to see God. Atheism has no eye with which to see, and no ear with which to hear, consequently it sees nothing and hears nothing. Just this is all the significance there is in the testimony of atheists. For when men proclaim their atheism and their infidelity with such vehemency as characterizes many of the harangues and essays now so popular in certain quarters, it will be found after all that they are not so much talking about divine things as exhibiting their own spiritual poverty. They think they are saying, and it may be demonstrating, that there is no God, and no Son of God, and no immortality, and no conscious life and blessedness awaiting human beings in the great realms beyond; but what they are really making clear is that their own spiritual natures are shriveled and atrophied. This was the pathetic confession of Darwin — that spiritual apprehensions and sensibilities had died out of him. His mind had become obscured to the fact and nearness of God.

A man must start with such faith as he has. If the faith is weak it is not to be despised; it is to be cherished and cultivated. But the simpler and more unquestioning the faith, the richer and ampler will be the responses. A little faith rightly used will grow to more faith, and the more to more still, till the answers to it are like the floodings of light in a June morning. No man knows to what heavenly splendors his eyes may be opened if he will only cultivate and cherish faith. No man knows how he may be filled with God if he will only believe with a steadily increasing energy.

> The childlike faith, that asks not sight,
>   Waits not for wonder or for sign,
> Believes, because it loves aright,
>   Shall see things greater, things divine.
> Heaven to that gaze shall open wide,
>   And brightest angels to and fro
> On messages of love shall glide,
>   'Twixt God above and heart below.

2. *It is men and women who value and use the knowledge they already have of God and spiritual realities who will be sure to make constant progress in this knowledge.*

There is a spiritual power which it is possible for devout souls to master. But it takes time and un-remitting effort to rise into these high masteries of things divine. It cannot be done in a moment, nor at a single leap.

God sometimes seems to break in on men, as on Paul, and suddenly arrest them in their mad careers, and show them the truth in such fullness as well-nigh to blind the soul with excess of light. This was done on the Day of Pentecost. Multitudes felt the sharp pressure of what seemed to them the divine finger on their consciences, and they turned about and came instantly into those sacred and lofty experiences which made it ever after easier to believe. But these are only apparent exceptions. The men who were so wrought upon on the Day of Pentecost were largely "devout men." They had in them the beginnings of knowledge.

Wider and surer knowledge, however, must come from the use of such knowledge as we have. Using such knowledge as we have will surely bring the wider and surer knowledge. What advances Peter and James and John made in spiritual apprehension! How much further along in right conceptions of God's thoughts and ways was the beloved Disciple on the Isle of Patmos than when, along with his associates, he wanted fire brought down on the village of the Samaritans!

In these times, when the air is full of misgivings and doubts, how refreshing it is to read the Great Apostle's repeated assertion, "We know." Paul "knew" that if the earthly house of this tabernacle were dissolved, there is yet another house for us yonder in the heavens. He "knew" that all things, under the providence of Him who notes the fall of a sparrow and numbers the hairs of our heads, work together for good to them that love God. He "knew" whom he believed. Indeed, he came to "know" things quite beyond the power of even his marvelous gift of speech to utter.

This wide reach of attainments and this altitude of positive assurance do not come by chance. They come by adding fact to fact. They come by pressing on from experience to experience. They come through a patient searching of the Word. They come through the communion of the closet. They come from having an ear attent to each fresh whisper of the Spirit. They come from making every new truth learned of God a round of the ladder on which to mount to still higher truths.

It is often amazing and always painful to see how little large numbers of men really get on in this deep and precious knowledge of God. They remind one of tourists who sometimes travel in foreign countries, amidst palaces, amidst towns and cities resplendent, amidst magnificent mountains and lakes, along rivers the most beautiful, and over grounds of intense historical interest, but who bring back only stories of petty personal annoyance in their comings and goings. Men walk back and forth amidst the multitudinous tokens of God, and right into the face of the splendors with which He illuminates the world, and yet they fail to recognize His presence and influence. His voice falls on their ears, and His hand beckons, and His Spirit is ready to co-work with all the faculties of the soul, and His providence is full of suggestion and ministry; but for all this they never get beyond the rudiments of Christian thinking and living. They never have anything to tell of rare and uplifting visions of God and of excursions into higher realms of light and joy. They never move forward into deeper convictions and larger views of Jesus Christ.

It is present knowledge cherished and nursed and cultivated; it is present knowledge increased by every possible method of enlargement, which will advance one till doubt after doubt is dissolved, and a thousand supposed mysteries are laid open, and the lofty disclosures of prophets and apostles and rapt seers are no longer either unintelligible or incredible. One comes to know even that which passes knowledge.

3. *Love also grows through the exercise of love.*

The more we love God and the things which are dear to the heart of God, the larger becomes our capacity for loving and the greater our satisfaction in loving. It is to loving souls that the divine love answers back in swelling tides of love. We love Him because He first loved us. He awakens love in our hearts, and sets the pulses of love in motion. He draws us out by expressions of love. But it is love in us which interprets love in Him; and the more we love the more we may love, and the better we may understand God. Madame Guyon is right when she says God can

> . . . not be dear
> When self engrosses all the thought;
> And groans and murmurs make it clear
> What else is loved the Lord is not.

At first the love may be very feeble; but if it be fostered, and currents for its free flowing be opened, it will become the controlling passion of the life.

This applies alike to the filial love of God and the benevolent love of men. The world's way is hate for hate and blow for blow. But when a man begins in sincerity and good earnest to love, and follows on where the spirit of love leads, he soon comes under the sweet dominion of a love which is large enough to embrace his enemies. What a measureless love was that which enabled the Divine Redeemer to exclaim on the cross: "Father, forgive them; for they know not what they do." But this love was echoed by the first martyr to the faith when he prayed: "Lord, lay not this sin to their charge." The fountains of love may be dried up in the soul by inaction and selfishness; or by a wise care in keeping them open they may be made to flow out in a steadily increasing volume. It is because they cultivated their love for God and man, and kept it in wholesome activity, that the pages of history are brightened with such names as Paul and Augustine and Eliot and Wilberforce and Howard and Mary Lyon and Emily Judson and Florence Nightingale and David Livingstone and John G. Paton of the New Hebrides.

In this way we might follow on around the entire circle of our spiritual capacities, and the result would be the same. It is the seeing eye to which things are revealed. It is the hearing ear to which things are spoken. The way to see more clearly, the way to hear more distinctly, is to be obedient to every voice and to every vision. The buried talent is withdrawn. The unused faculty withers. To him that hath shall be given; but from him that hath not shall be taken away. Only by the use, wise and persistent, of those faculties by which we know God, and serve God, and walk in the fellowship of God, shall we ever be able to realize the sublime aspirations of the Apostle when he said: "I count not myself yet to have apprehended; but one thing I do, forgetting the things which are behind, and stretching forward to the things which are before, I press on toward the goal unto the prize of the high calling of God in Christ Jesus."

> There went a man from home; and to his neighbors twain
> He gave to keep for him, two sacks of golden grain.
> Deep in his cellar one the precious charge concealed;
> And forth the other went and strewed it in his field.
> The man returns at last — asks of the first his sack;
> 'Here, take it; 'tis the same; thou hast it safely back.'
> Unharmed it shows without; but when he would explore
> His sack's recesses, corn there finds he now no more;
> One half of what was there proves rotten and decayed,
> Upon the other half have worm and mildew preyed.
> The putrid heap to him in ire he doth return,
> Then of the other asks: 'Where is my sack of corn?'
> Who answered: 'Come with me and see how it has sped,'
> And took and showed him fields with waving harvest spread.'
>   TRENCH.

OUR INSUFFICIENCY MADE SUFFICIENT IN GOD.

Who is sufficient for these things?   2 Cor. 2: 16.
Our sufficiency is from God.   2 Cor. 3: 5.

THESE two passages, brought together in this way, disclose to us, even before it can be announced, the theme of the morning, which is: *Our Insufficiency Made Sufficient in God.*

Paul was speaking of his ministry.   The imagery chosen, according to Professor Plumptre in Ellicott's Commentary, through which to express his thought was "that of the solemn triumphal procession of a Roman emperor or general."   He conceived of himself as one who had been conquered by the grace of God in Christ and was being led along, a willing captive, in the ranks of those who were attached to the chariot of the Divine Victor.   "But thanks be unto God, which always leadeth us in triumph in Christ."

This, however, was not the whole of it.   He added: "And maketh manifest through us the savour of His knowledge in every place."   Evidently, to follow still the guidance of the scholar already named, this was said with reference to the incense which was an essential part of each Roman triumph.   The words he spoke in testimony of the redeeming love and power of Jesus were "incense-clouds," so he seemed to fashion the matter to his own mind, which bore to all around, as they were wafted in the air, tidings that the Conqueror had come, laden with tokens of His subduing might.

But the use of this analogy suggested a more serious aspect of the case. For some who appeared in those Roman triumphs were on their way to a glad deliverance, while some were on their way to disgrace and death. All to whom the knowledge of Christ came through the preaching of the Apostle, were to be sharers in the incense of the knowledge; but not all, like himself and whoever else might believe, were to be victorious captives. "For we are a sweet savour of Christ unto God, in them that are being saved, and in them that are perishing; to the one a savour from death unto death; to the other a savour of life unto life." Or as our expositor has said: "To some" his holding forth of salvation through a crucified Redeemer "would seem to be as a breath from paradise, giving life and health; to another its sweetness would seem sickly and pestilential, coming as from a charnel house, having in it the savour of death and leading to death as its issue."

Well might the Apostle follow up these statements with the question: "Who is sufficient for these things?" Well might any one whose business it is to handle the truth of God, whether as a preacher or teacher or most inconspicuous worker, put the question. For the outcome of efforts in the sphere of winning souls into the faith of the Son of God, is simply beyond the power of estimate in human speech. It is touching, it is more than touching — it is to the last degree instructive to see this man with his massive intellect, with his trained faculties, with his stores of knowledge and with his experience and courage, falling back into such a profound sense of his own insufficiency.

But Paul quickly came upon an answer to his question. It was not in himself, nor in his associates, nor in any scheme of stoicism or desperation, that he could find the required sufficiency. It was in God. In God he could go bravely and successfully on. "Who is sufficient for these things?" "Not of ourselves; our sufficiency is from God."

This truth, so exactly suited to the needs of Paul, and to all who have come after him in the ministry of the Word, has a yet wider application than to preachers and to the work in which preachers are engaged. There is no one who stands face to face with any serious task in life, in whom it would not be becoming and profitable to turn the eye inward and take the measure of his qualifications for what he is to do. There is no one who stands face to face with any serious task in life, who might not fitly harbor distrust of his ability to discharge in the wisest and best way the duties committed to his hands, and in terms of deepest sincerity and earnestness cry out for a higher sufficiency.

With what eminent propriety might every mother,

on taking a new-born babe into her arms, exclaim in accents of unfeigned solicitude: "Who is sufficient for the lofty service of training this immortal soul so that whatever of evil tendency there is in it by nature shall be corrected or suppressed, and whatever of good, actual or possible, shall be developed, and there shall be no missing of the sublime destiny open to it through the wisdom and love of God?"

With what striking suitableness, too, might fathers join in with mothers and ask: "How is this group of children who are gradually gathering about our hearth-stone and our table, and who will so quickly push on through youth to mature years, to be kept sweet and loving and lovable, and so educated in the faith of Jesus, and all the principles and aims and excellencies for which the name of Jesus stands, that they may be not alone our children, but in their hearts God's children, ready to walk in His light, and glad always to do His divine will?"

The teacher in our public schools and in our various institutions of learning, meeting pupils day by day in any worthy consciousness of the influence necessarily exerted by one who performs the sacred function of instructor, and of the tenacious way in which this influence will abide in all the years to come; the physician who goes about amongst his patients at all hours, burdened as he often must be with the feeling that the issues of life and death hang on his insight and skill and fidelity; the editor who pens words sure to be factors in shaping individual sentiment and molding public opinion, and so to be marked helps or hindrances to the progress and happiness of society, might each be pardoned not only, but commended in warmest phrase, for pausing now and then and solemnly asking: "Who is sufficient for these things?"

There would be more ground for hope that the men who aspire to places of trust and honor in the public service — who want to be aldermen and mayors and governors and representatives and senators and judges and cabinet officers and presidents, and who succeed in reaching these responsible positions — would discharge their duties a great deal better, whether of translating the deliberate thought of the masses of the people into law, or of interpreting the law in courts of justice, or of executing law in the interest of the common welfare, if they only had a somewhat profounder sense, or in many instances any sense at all, of their own insufficiency for meeting demands so grave. For these civil duties, viewed either from the standpoint of an intelligent obligation to God or humanity, are high and exacting. It is refreshing to go back and see how this sense of self-insufficiency pervaded the minds of some of the great founders of our Republic.

Now the value of this sense of insufficiency, as Paul felt it, and as it ought to be felt by all, in all spheres of life, who are charged with any kind of grave responsibility, is that it drives men back to the true source of sufficiency. It drives them back to

Him in whom alone are to be found the love and wis-dom and patience and strength actually needed for the work laid upon them.

It is not that men are not to be self-reliant as against the peculiar feeling of dependence which cuts all the nerves of resolution. It is not that men are not to move forward in a spirit of determined aggressiveness as against standing still and merely marking time. It is not that men are not to be cour-ageous, and ready to assume fitting attitudes on all questions of moment as against the timidity and cowardice which never venture on any risks, or the undertaking of any enterprise which calls for the ex-ercise of a strong faith. But it is that men, on the one hand, shall have such a conviction of the sacred-ness and far-reaching influence of the work which has been committed to them to do, and such a whole-some distrust, on the other hand, of their own capa-bilities and preparation, that they will be constrained to fall on their knees and implore God to grant the divine inner girding and divine guidance required to fill up the measure of ability.

There is nothing so harmful, unless one crosses the border-line and launches out into a career of open immorality and vice, as self-conceit. Let one start out with the idea that he knows it all, and can do it all, without much aid from men, and with none at all from God, in virtue of his own superior wit or insight, and he will be more than likely to come to grief. What sorry collapses there have been in the home world, and in the literary world, and in the political and reform world, and in the religious world, because men thought they were sufficient in themselves, and could get on without God! How insignificant and painful — not to say ridiculous — in instances not a few, has been the outcome of efforts which were begun with flaming manifestoes and blare of trumpets and the ostentatious announcement that short work was to be made of revolutionizing the world and turning all mankind over to peace and plenty and virtue!

No matter what wealth of knowledge a man may have, nor what resources, nor what numbers he can rally to his support, it is never wise to leave God out of the reckoning. In no home, in no school, in no senate-chamber, in no reform circle, in no church, is there enough of wisdom and strength to meet all the responsibilities and discharge all the duties in a way to secure the "well-done" of the Master at last, without supplement from God. Apart from God, nothing aright. In God, all things.

One of the reasons, no doubt, why there is so little sense of our insufficiency, or need of the light and help of God, is that life, to our ordinary average thought, is not invested with the sanctity which belongs to it. We cut up life, as we do time, into sections, and then say this little bit of a section is sacred, but the rest may go to such uses as we choose without any feeling of accountability. Life in the length and breadth of it, life in all the belongings and outgoings of it, life in its totality, is not set over into the sunlight of the divine estimate, and measured back from the gateway of eternity. The inspired view of life involves creation in the image of God, an immortal destiny, and the possibility of unlimited development in knowledge and virtue. The inspired view of life involves the doing of everything as under the great Taskmaster's eye. "Whether, therefore, ye eat, or drink, or whatever ye do, do all to the glory of God." No man's conception of life is properly elevated until, in the whole sweep of it, it is brought up and put under the rule of the "glory of God," or, what comes to the same thing in effect, the rule of "the love of God."

Keble has a hymn in which he intimates that the "trivial round" and the "common task" of life will furnish all one may reasonably desire in the way of opportunity for self-denial and advancing in nearness to the Father. This never seemed to me to be quite true. But it is true that the "trivial round" and the "common task" may be illuminated, and ought to be, with the thought that God can be served in them, and that these small activities can be made a means of grace to the soul. Such a thought sanctifies the "round" and the "task," and they are no longer "trivial" and "common." For as our author sings in the same hymn:

> If in our daily course our mind
> Be set, to hallow all we find,
> New treasures still, of countless price,
> God will provide for sacrifice.

Old friends, old scenes, will lovelier be,
As more of heaven in each we see;
Some softening gleam of love and prayer
Shall dawn on every cross and care.

It matters not that multitudes use life as though it were simply a prolonged banquet, and that eating and drinking and wild dissipation sum up its meaning; nor that other multitudes use it as though it were something to be bartered away in exchange for houses and lands and heaps of gold; nor that still other multitudes use it till it is worn out in chafing and fretting against its mysteries and limitations. Life is yet something superlatively regal. It is a beam whose sun is the great central orb of the moral universe. It is a stream whose fountain is the source of all intelligence and joy. It is a song, if only we will let it sing itself out, whose key-note was struck by Him who attuned the melody of the morning stars. What it may become, how rare, how exalted, is shown in the Divine Man.

Another of the reasons, no doubt, why there is little sense of our insufficiency, or need of the light and help of God, is that we do not set our hands to tasks which tax energy, intellectual, moral, spiritual and sympathetic alike, to the utmost, and make us stand aghast and tremble in view of possible failure. Paul would never have had the oppressive feeling of his own inability which made him cry out: "Who is sufficient for these things?" had he not been engaged in a service whose effects for good or ill he saw in so many instances to be immediate, and whose issues he knew, in any event, would be endless. He was under the strain of an effort to make known the saving grace of God in Christ all up and down the lands; and it put every faculty and every power of his nature to the test. He threw down the gauntlet to prejudice and superstition and sin, and the conflict had not been long on before he discovered that it calls for something beyond human skill and force to meet such foes. He was committed to a task which revealed his own weakness.

Otherwise he would not have known it. For it is not when a man sits in some sunny nook, or lolls in a hammock on an August day, chatting, sleeping, reading novels, or dreaming dreams, that he will be likely to have a tormenting sense of his own incapacity to do difficult things. There is nothing before him to which he is not equal, — why get excited and toss and fret? It is when a man undertakes to lift a heavy weight that he finds out whether he has any strength or not. It is when a man undertakes to run a race, and is pushed from start to finish by eager and trained competitors, that he finds out how well his muscles are developed, and whether he has any staying qualities in him. It is when a man undertakes to play a musical instrument, or to solve a hard problem in mathematics, or to try a case in court, or to conduct a diplomatic negotiation, that he finds out — or if he does not, others do for him — whether he is up to the demands of these several duties, or is wholly lacking in the needed ability.

Some people have never felt their insufficiency in wrestling with an easily besetting sin, because they have never faced an easily besetting sin in the determination to conquer it or die in the attempt. They lie on their oars and drift with the current of their own inclinations or impulses or habits, and so long as they do this they have no idea of the strength required to row against the current. Coleridge made this discovery very soon when he undertook to stop the use of opium. He did not know the strength of the cords by which he was bound till he tried to break them. It is the same with almost any man given over to evil indulgence. It is hard to cut loose from any dominant passion; and unless God helps, or one is willing to lay hold on the help of God, there is little ground for hope.

Some people have never felt their insufficiency in guiding a soul into the faith of Christ, because they have never tried to do this kind of work. They have never felt their insufficiency in the business of lifting a community to a higher level of thinking and acting, because they have never lent a hand to endeavors looking to this end. They have never felt their insufficiency in overcoming some definite form of evil, and doing their best to rid the world of it, because they have never stood front to front with any definite form of evil, and openly and bravely challenged it to mortal combat. Quite likely there may be large numbers who fancy that they have enough wisdom and strength and grace to perform, in short order, the tasks under which others seem to be sweating and staggering, if only they were to turn attention to them, who would speedily change their estimate of themselves and their competency for difficult undertakings, were they to make a few experiments.

The matter is that our views of the difficulties involved in overcoming evil in any of its forms and making things better, are keyed too low. Let a man fairly commit himself to some moral enterprise — to some movement which is clearly for the good of mankind and the glory of God, but which can be made successful only by counter-matching cunning with truth, and stirring up vast bulks of indifference, and dislodging selfishness from strongholds in which it has been long maintained, and it will not be long before he will be impressed with a feeling of his own littleness and impotency. The wonder in his mind will come to be, not why so many hold back or lose heart, but why anybody has the courage to pit his small allotment of wisdom and energy against wrongs so shrewd and persistent and gigantic. It would seem a little thing to get sin out of a single human heart, to persuade just one soul to break with wickedness, and turn the back on iniquity; but is it? Do we find it so?

Many things, it is true, seem to be done with comparative ease. These things are done by men who do not pretend to look to God for guidance, and whose doings frequently fill the world with noise. But these doings cut no figure in the world's moral progress. The thought now in mind is of the things which are pre-eminently worth doing. It is of the things which save and bless souls, which save and bless communities and states and races, and which uplift and advance humanity. All this costs and often baffles and appalls. No man can work long in these high spheres and for these holy ends without a sense of need which will constrain him to break out with the question: "Who is sufficient for these things?" The urgency and frequency of this cry will measure appreciation of the difficulties to be overcome.

The encouraging side of this truth is that just as soon as a man becomes sensible of his insufficiency, and really desires a wisdom and strength adequate to the duties he has to discharge, God will be to him the sufficiency he needs. He will come in upon him in forms of light and courage and moral energy.

When God appeared to Moses in the flame of the burning bush at Horeb, and laid upon him the unprecedented responsibility of leadership in delivering the children of Israel from their hard Egyptian bondage, this large providential man, who was to loom into such majestic proportions that his name and fame would fill all the centuries, shrank back and said: "Who am I?" It is the same as though he had asked: "What fitness is there in me for this extraordinary undertaking?" He was only a shepherd, leading the flocks of his father-in-law, Jethro, back and forth in the wilderness of Midian, and it seemed like mockery to summon him to this great service. Urged still further, his reply was substantially the same: "O Lord, I am not eloquent, neither heretofore, nor since Thou hast spoken unto Thy servant; for I am slow of speech and of a slow tongue." To his own thought he had no competency to make pleas in behalf of justice and freedom before Pharaoh, and to persuade a down-trodden people, like the Israelites, that he could secure their emancipation. But this was the immortal answer to his objection: "Who hath made man's mouth? Or who maketh man dumb, or deaf, or seeing, or blind? Is it not I, the Lord? Now, therefore, go, and I will be with thy mouth, and teach thee what thou shalt speak." Here was hesitancy; here was timidity; here was even a painful sense of insufficiency; but God said: "Look to Me; I will take your insufficiency, and in my divine wisdom and strength make it sufficient." He did; and the man so girded and directed went forth to one of the most memorable achievements of all the ages.

How different would have been the issue had Moses been a man full of pride and self-conceit! When called and appointed of God to this unique service, suppose he had said: "Oh yes, I can do it; I have sympathy with my people in their distresses; I know human nature; I am instructed in all the wisdom of the Egyptians· and out in this wilderness with the flocks, and under the stars, and in the midst of wild roving bands, both my body and my mind have become seasoned to patient endurance, and I can do it." What would have been the result? In the first place he would not have been called to this position. In the second place, even though he had been called, and this great and sacred duty had been laid upon him, he would not have turned to God for the proper furnishing for his work and hence would surely have failed. For neither Moses nor any other man could ever carry through to its final consummation an undertaking so prodigious as this without aid from the wisdom and strength of God.

The same hesitation and shrinking are discovered in Jeremiah. God had a very peculiar and difficult work for this old prophet to do. Amongst all the great names which figure in biblical story there is not one, perhaps, which is so little understood and so imperfectly appreciated. His mission was indicated to him; but he met it with a protest; he was not equal to it. From the narrative we should infer that the man was thrown into something like torture when told what was expected of him. Instantly and instinctively he said: "Not I! Not I! I am not sufficient for these things." But just this was the way to become sufficient. His sense of insufficiency was such that God could enter into him and be his sufficiency in all the ways of counsel and courage and holy might.

The Apostle's statement, therefore, that he did not feel himself to be sufficient for these things which were laid upon him, but that he found his sufficiency in God, is at once the culmination and the prophecy of all experience in the higher departments of religious activity. There is no other explanation of the tremendous changes which have been wrought in the world along the line of reform and the setting up of the kingdom of Christ. Weak men, as the world judges, men without the advantages of wealth and social position, and sometimes with very little of the cultivation of the schools, have often been mighty to the pulling down of strongholds. There is not a nation in the world, nor a church, whose history does not confirm the assertion that a few souls, illuminated with the divine wisdom and girded with the divine might, are more than a match for all the foes that can be marshaled against them. Recall such triumphs as those of Gideon and his band.

May not the assertion be ventured that the one supreme demand of our times is for men and women so emptied of self — so deeply and painfully conscious of their own insufficiency for the duties laid upon them — that God can enter into them, and fill them with the light and energy of His Spirit? This is an age of organization and machinery. If it occurs to anybody to do anything, instead of doing it, he starts a society. We rely on bulk and numbers and moral standing. What is needed beyond everything else is to fall back into reliance on God. It is the wheel in which we trust rather than the spirit within the wheel. There will be strength in the church of Christ, and courage and a spirit of aggressiveness, more nearly correspondent with the length of our membership rolls and the wealth represented in our communicants, when there is a deeper sense that all real sufficiency must be found where the great Apostle found it, not in ourselves but in God. "I will strengthen thee" is the divine promise, and the human testimony is: "I can do all things in Him that strengtheneth me."

FAITH AND WORKS.

For as the body apart from the spirit is dead, even so faith apart from works is dead. James 2: 26.

THE topic for the morning is: *Faith and Works.* The task imposed by the topic is to make somewhat clearer, if possible, the mutual relations of the two ideas and duties.

Had this book of James never been written, and were some man of the present day, having the strength of the Apostle, and looking at truth from his standpoint, and feeling, as he did, the need of more Christian activity, to write it out and give it to the world, word for word, exactly as we find it, there is no doubt a great many people would fall upon it and try to tear it into shreds and patches. In their eagerness to maintain the form of sound words they would not only denounce it as lacking in a clear, full statement of Christian doctrine, but as being, in some particulars, in direct antagonism to the fundamental teaching of the Gospel. As it is — a book of the New Testament, having on it the seal of inspiration, and bearing down to us abundant authentication of its genuineness, Martin Luther did not hesitate to say it was wanting in "all evangelical character." In comparison with the Epistles of Paul, and the

other New Testament writings, he called it "a verita-
ble straw epistle."

But this simply shows that God's revelation is for
the ages, and, in its many-sided completeness, is not
infrequently more than any one man can master or
can hold.   The great soul of the German reformer,
from the nature of the case, was all on fire with the
cardinal doctrine of faith.   In him faith was just
what James took so much pains to say all faith ought
to be — a living and fruitful principle. While he himself failed to appreciate the idea, openly and fiercely
arrayed himself against the idea, that any emphasis
is to be placed on good works, those who have come
after him, and have entered into his triumphant labors, see clearly that the life he lived was well-nigh
an ideal exemplification of the instruction he belittled.
Luther turned from James and clung to Paul; but
in the working out of his convictions, as they were
inspired by Paul, and in his rugged victories for God
and man, he illustrated precisely and most manfully
the vital meanings of James.   In Luther, as in Abraham and in all true, heroic souls, we see, not one
Apostle over against another, but both together; not
faith and works in conflict, but faith and works in
the harmonious relations of cause and effect, of seed
and fruit, of principle and principle applied.

Here we lay bare the secret of the whole matter.
There are no irreconcilable differences between
Paul and James, but both are consistent because both
are true.   Paul says: "Have faith."   "Yes," says

James, "have faith; but see to it that it is a living faith." Paul says: "Let no man put his trust for salvation in the works of the law." "Yes," says James again, "but let him remember that faith as well as the law has works, and the only way in which faith can be shown to be saving is by its working." This is only another way of saying that faith to be faith must be a faith that works by love and purifies the heart.

Paul felt this just as much as James, for he said it over and over again; just as James felt the need and value of faith equally with Paul, for this is the assumption on which his whole epistle was built. Paul looked at men as sinners, and he said: "No amount of work will save sinners; it must be of grace through faith in the Lord Jesus Christ." James looked at men as believers already in the fellowship of Jesus, and he said: "This believing — this believing as a mere intellectual operation, just as a devil may believe even to trembling, will do no good without corresponding activity." Paul was dealing chiefly with the two thoughts of grace and sin. James was dealing chiefly with the two thoughts of knowing and doing. Their points of view were not just the same.

This letter of James, indeed, might be considered a practical discourse founded on the words of our Lord: "If ye know these things, happy are ye if ye do them." For see how in the first chapter he falls into line with the Master's thought, and reproduces it in almost exact form. "But be ye doers of the Word, and not hearers only, deluding your own selves." Nor was he content simply to say this, but he enforced it with illustrations: "For if any one is a hearer of the Word, and net a doer, he is like unto a man beholding his natural face in a mirror; for he beholdeth himself and goeth and straightway forgetteth what manner of man he was. But he that looketh into the perfect law, the law of liberty, and so continueth, being not a hearer that forgetteth, but a doer that worketh, this man shall be blessed in his doing."

With Paul faith is an energy that must of necessity produce results. How strongly he puts this: "For in Jesus Christ neither circumcision availeth anything, nor uncircumcision." Mere forms, that is, of religious observances, so long as they are mere forms and nothing else, have no value — "but faith which worketh by love." With James, on the other hand, works are a result which demonstrate the existence and activity of faith. "Yea, a man will say, thou hast faith and I have works; show me thy faith apart from thy works, and I by my works will show thee my faith."

In this way it was, the Father of the faithful could stand as the type of the doctrine of each. Paul saw in Abraham one who was justified by a faith which was a working faith. James saw in Abraham one who was justified by the working of faith. Augustine brings out the thought exactly when he says: "The faith of Abraham was imputed to him for righteousness, before it had brought forth works; but it was a living faith, in which the works lay as to the germ." He calls a faith which has no work in it "a palsied hand."

Works then, it may be safely taken for granted, have a very vital and important relation to this matter of personal acceptability with God. As having a decidedly significant and, as it seems to me, a conclusive bearing on this point, let me call attention to this one fact — the marked contrast, in form, between the conditions laid down for entering into the Christian life, and the ground on which final judgment, in almost every instance, is represented as turning.

As to the teachings we have, and the instances given in illustration of the teaching, concerning the way of entering on this new, divine life, there is no need of any elaborate statement. It is all summed up in the one word "believe." Over and over again did Christ declare that men become His disciples by believing. "Whosoever believeth" is the formulary of admission into the Christian life. The preaching of the Apostles was uniform in this particular. The Book of Acts makes this clear. No matter what a man's moral condition, his history, position, nationality, vocation, previous creed, age, social relations, the one thing insisted on was belief in Jesus. Faith was declared to be the open gateway through which men were to walk into the hopes of a blessed immortality. Sometimes it is called "faith in His

name," sometimes "faith in His blood," sometimes
"faith in Christ," or "faith in the Son of God," but
it is always faith; faith going out to and centering in
the Divine Person of Jesus. What Paul says to the
Ephesians is the statement which covers all the in-
structions: "For by grace are ye saved through faith."
No man with the New Testament before him may an-
nounce any other condition, or any additional condition. "Come unto Me, all ye that labor and are
heavy laden, and I will give you rest." "Whosoever will, let him take the water of life freely."

Passing from the beginning to the end; from the
representation of the condition on which the new life
in God is begun, to the consideration which determines
the award in the final judgment, we find the accent
changed. It is not so much faith that is emphasized
as character. Listen to Paul: "Wherefore we labor
that whether present or absent we may be accepted
of Him. For we must all appear before the judgment seat of Christ, that every one may receive the
things done in his body, according to that he hath
done, whether good or bad." God is one, so the same
Apostle tells us, "who will render to every man according to his deeds." The stress is laid on deeds — on
what one has done and has come to be. In other
words, character is made to be the standard of judgment. In this respect John is at one with Paul:
"Seal not the sayings of the prophecy of this Book,
for the time is at hand — he that is unjust let him be
unjust still; and he which is filthy let him be filthy

still; and he that is righteous let him be righteous still; and he that is holy let him be holy still. And behold I come quickly, and My reward is with Me to give to every man according as his work shall be. Blessed are they that do His commandments, that they may have right to the tree of life, and may enter in through the gates into the city. For without are dogs and sorcerers and whoremongers and murderers and idolatars, and whosoever loveth and maketh a lie." Character, just what a man has wrought himself into, settles the question of his destiny. Has he been just or unjust? Clean or filthy? These are the questions with which one is to be met at the great day. This is exactly the way Jesus forecasts the final issue. 'I was an hungered and ye gave Me meat; thirsty, and ye gave Me drink; a stranger, and ye took Me in; naked, and ye clothed Me; sick, and ye visited Me; in prison, and ye came unto Me; so inherit the kingdom prepared for you from the foundation of the world.' It was things done — things done until they were incorporated into character. "I was an hungered and ye gave Me no meat; thirsty, and ye gave Me no drink; a stranger, and ye took Me not in; naked, and ye clothed Me not; sick and in prison, and ye visited Me not; so go to your own place and to your own associations." It was things not done — not done until they became the expression and register of the real moral state of the soul. Not a word about faith; it is all about works. No word of praise is given, and no word of fault is uttered, on the basis of what has been believed or not believed. What one believes or does not believe is not made the basis of the reward, it is what one has done. Have you done this thing or not?

In what way, now, is all this to be reconciled? One state of mind or attitude exalted at the beginning — apparently another at the end. One condition declared to be a necessity at the start — something else emphasized at the close, and that which was so necessary at the outset not so much as mentioned. When one *comes in*, the simple question is: "*Do you believe?*" If so, entrance is not disputed. When one *goes out* the question is: "*What have you done?*" If nothing, then it is all over with him. The reconciliation is found precisely where James located it. It is found in the statement that "faith apart from works is dead." Or what is the same thing, faith apart from works is no faith at all. There is no shifting of ground. It is not maintained that faith, after the initial step, is of no further consequence to one. All through, at the beginning, middle and end, faith is of all consequence. But a faith which does not carry consecration in it, and embrace head and hand and heart and all substance is really not faith. It may be a full mental assent, it may have in it the form of sound words, but a living faith and a loving faith it surely is not. Faith must be all-inclusive of a man, a controlling force in him, out-reaching energy, life, before it can be a justifying

faith. A simple, easy-going, technical utterance of
the phrase, "I believe," is not going to waft anybody
over into God's kingdom. It takes a different kind
of wing to soar away to the heavenly gates.

Here is a hungry man before you, and you have
the means to feed him; but instead of feeding him
you say: "Oh, I believe, I believe." No, you don't
believe, and God will spew you out for pretending
to believe. Here is a man naked, and you can clothe
him if you will; but instead of clothing him you say:
"Oh, I believe, I believe." No, you don't believe,
and God will send you shivering out of His presence. Here are the sick needing sympathy, minis-
tration, treatment, care, and over and above all the
ordinary obligations of life is the duty of helping
them; but you say: "Oh, I believe, I believe." No,
you don't believe, and God will say: "Get thee behind Me with all such faith, for it is no faith, but a
sham." Here is a great world to be operated on in
the interest of truth and purity and justice and the setting up of the kingdom of Christ; all of which means
somebody's thought and somebody's prayers and
somebody's time and strength and money — means
each man's thought and prayers and time and strength
and money, after the measure of his ability; but any
attempt to evade these obligations and duties
on the ground that one can articulate the formulary of belief, and that that is enough, will be
met with the same assertion that this is not belief. Persons taking this attitude simply deceive

themselves. They are unprofitable servants, and God will not own them. Faith means one's best endeavors after the mind that was in Christ, and to work the will of Christ. "Not every one that saith unto Me, Lord, Lord, shall enter into the kingdom of heaven, but he that doeth the will of My Father which is in heaven."

With the general subject of faith and works opened out in this way, we are now ready for certain instructive and practical inferences which it will be worth our while to treasure.

I. *Works — good works — are the natural issue of a living faith.*

A living faith moves right on to good works as a matter of course, and in them is consummated. Just as waters pour out from living fountains, just as light and warmth from the sun, just as fragrance from a fresh blossom, just as vegetation springs from seed planted in a fertile soil, just as a song from a bird's throat, or rain from an over-full cloud, or a poem from a surcharged poet's soul, or beneficence and loving kindness and tender mercies from the great heart of God, — so activities looking to one's own purifying and growth in grace and knowledge, and services in behalf of every good interest and of every righteous cause, are the normal, and not only normal but inevitable, outcome of a living faith. A living faith has to show itself in this way. This is why, if a man has faith equal to a grain of mustard seed, he can remove mountains. A living faith is dynamic.

It grows, and as it grows it overturns things. Martin Luther says, and in this saying he pays an unconscious tribute to the James he sought to belittle: "Oh, faith is a lively, busy, active thing, so that it is impossible for it not to be ceaselessly working good. It does not ask either if good works are to be done, but before it asks it has done them, and is ever doing. But whoso doeth not such work is an unbelieving man — gropes and looks out for faith and good works, and neither knows what is faith, nor what are good works, but for all, chatters and talks much of faith and good works. Faith is a living, well-weighed assurance of the grace of God. . . . Hence, a man having this faith becomes, without constraint, ready and glad to serve everybody, to suffer many things to the praise of God who has been so gracious to him, so that it is impossible to separate works from faith, yea, as impossible as it is to separate burning and shining from fire."

II. *Works — good works — are the demonstration of faith.*

How many times a man, especially a man who is above the average in earnestness and conscientiousness, asks the question: "Well, now, am I really a disciple of Jesus Christ, a child of God, an heir to the everlasting inheritance, one who has passed from death unto life; or am I deceiving my own soul, and cherishing hopes which I have no right to entertain?" He turns his views over, and looks at them. He examines his feelings, and wonders if they are of the right sort. But the true test is the outcome. If a man has the faith which allies the soul to God, there will be evidence of it in his acting. There will be both the spirit and the habit of benefi- cence. It will come out in a temper of self-sacrifice and serviceableness. If one, knowing that there has been a moment in his life when he turned to God with full purpose of heart, can see the natural fruit- age of faith, he may rest content. It is the tendency of faith to go out, to go abroad, and to keep doing this till it is itself covered up, and possibly lost sight of in results.

Here is a little seed; it is the seed of an apple; it is nothing but a seed. One can take it and hold it between thumb and finger. But what is in it? Plant it and see. For when it is planted in a suitable soil, and with a suitable exposure, there will come forth from it a trunk, branches, boughs, leaves, buds, blossoms and, in due time, bushels and bushels of sound, ripe, luscious apples. These are the things which lay back in germ in the little seed all the time. It only needed that opportunity should be given in order to set the tendencies in the seed on towards these results. But where is that seed now? Without the seed there would have been no tree, no apples; but where is the seed? One looks at the trunk, but there is no seed to be seen, and nothing like a seed. One looks at the branches, the twigs, the buds, the blossoms, the fruit, and still there is no trace of the seed. Cut the apple open and a seed will be found in it — a seed after its kind — but it is not the seed which was planted. From the moment the seed was planted it was lost sight of. The fruit is the demonstration of the seed. The fruit is the seed's end. The fruit is the thing which was wanted, and for which the seed was made to exist.

Faith is the seed. Everything lies wrapped up in faith. But works — good works — are the fruits. It is the fruits we are aiming at. It is the fruits which show us what the seed was. In the judgment the thing which God takes in hand and examines, and passes upon, is not the seed but the fruit. At the outset it was the seed; at the end it is the fruit. One's care at the beginning must be that the seed is good, and such as will unfold into good fruit. But it is the fruit which demonstrates the quality of the seed. It is the fruit on which we lay stress. It is the fruit we want; it is the fruit which God wants. When a man's life suggests Jesus, is after the type of Jesus, and is full of the good works of Jesus, it is very certain his faith in Jesus is of the right kind.

III.   *Works — good works — are the things which make our faith of value to the world.*

Good works, as we have seen, are the credentials of faith. But good works are the commendation of faith. If we want to carry our faith forward, and make it seem precious to men; if we want to make our faith a power in the world — a power to emancipate the bondaged and to lift humanity up; if we want to show forth the Lord Jesus Christ as lovable

and loving, and to invest the blessed name of our
Heavenly Father with attractiveness, it must be by
pushing our faith out into a sweet and practical efficiency. It must be made clear that our Gospel is a
Gospel of self-denial and helpfulness. We go far to
discredit the faith reposed in Jesus Christ in the estimation of men, and to dishonor the salvation we have
through this faith, when we are careless and selfish
in our practical living. Infidelity never has had and
does not have in our day any weapons so powerful
for evil as the inconsistencies and meannesses of
Christian men.

Let the time come when men and women who
have named the name of the Lord are careful to depart from iniquity; when they are so sensitive to evil
that the very suspicion of wrong fills them with pain;
when the mind that was in Christ is in them, and
they are self-denying for their fellow-men, and fond
of doing good; when they are no longer conformed
to this world, but are transformed by the renewing
power of the grace of the Holy Spirit; when, like
Paul, the life they live in the flesh is a life of faith
in the Son of God; when they make it a part of their
daily duty to reclaim and restore the wandering, to
help the needy, to aid in bearing the burdens of
those who are heavy laden through the misfortunes
of life or the allotments of Providence, — then the
skepticisms which are abroad, like so many owls and
bats, will betake themselves into the darkness. There
would be no gainsaying a faith which should be

commended to the world in millions of lives, at once
consistent from a moral standpoint, and all the time
flowing out in streams of beneficence.

This is worthy the most serious thought. There
is no advocacy of the faith to which we cling so
effective as earnest and consistent living. There
are no answers to the objections which men bring
against the Gospel so conclusive as the good deeds
done by those who believe in Christ. Just in the
ratio in which Christian men and women are only
nominally Christian, but are worldly, swayed by the
lusts and ambitions of the world, infidelity and immorality will come to the front. Just in the ratio in
which Christian men and women are pure and loving and helpful, infidelity and immorality will give
way, and our humanity will move on towards the
ideal; or, to put it all into a word, our faith must be
real in order to have any power in it. There is no
power, at best only a temporary semblance of power,
in any sort of a sham. A sham faith is amongst the
weakest and most contemptible of all the shams with
which the world is afflicted.

IV. *It is through good works, works, that is,
which are wrought in the spirit of love, that our own
faith is quickened and strengthened.*

We very often, and very fitly, pray for an increase
of faith. Nothing tends more surely to this than trying to do something which shall make men think of
the spirit that was in the Master. A word spoken
with no other thought than that it is for Jesus the

Lord; a deed done with no other aim than to be found in line with the interest of the Master, always reacts to the enlarging of our spiritual life.

This is the universal testimony and experience. Workers are always ready to testify that their faith is never so clear and strong as when they are diligently at service for the Son of God. They say: "At times when we are all absorbed in our Christian activities, the word of God seems more precious, the promises of God seem greater, salvation through a crucified Redeemer seems more than ever needful to men, and more than ever adapted to their actual necessities, and this whole vast realm of spiritual verity and life seems lighted up as with a new radiance from heaven." There are the common-sense and the logic of a true philosophy in it all. Action clarifies, action brushes the clouds out of the sky and clears the cobwebs out of the brain; action puts the whole moral system in a healthy condition, and one can see with new clearness.

Why, a man may listen, and listen, and listen forever, and not know so much about the truth in certain vital phases of it, as he can learn by one hour of faithful dealing with a soul that is deeply conscious of sin and is in earnest in the determination to be saved from sin. The twists and kinks men often get into their heads on theological points come partly because they are simply theorizers and not practical workers; and their eccentric and imperfect ideas grow out of their partial experiences.

It is not to be inferred from this that all men are to do the same kind of work. Far from it. Not all birds sing the same song. Not all trees yield the same fruit. Not all mines give forth the same precious metals. Not all fields wave with the same harvests. The law is individuality, variety. Not all are fitted for the same kind of work. There is one Spirit; but there are diversities of gifts. There is one kingdom; but the sphere and needs and opportunities of the kingdom are manifold. One can do one thing better — another another. One has his special service defined for him in his capabilities or his circumstances. Providence indicates another sort of service for somebody else. In the divine economy there is a place for each man and a man for each place; a work for each worker.

For one thing every man who has confessed Christ is to live his daily life, and do his daily work, in a way to magnify his Master's name. A man who does this, whether on farm or vessel, in store or mill, or making bricks, or driving nails, or shoving planes, or weaving cloths, or building houses and bridges, or teaching, or setting types, or surveying, or practicing law or medicine, or writing books — that is, does his work honestly, worthily, so that it can be said of it, it is a true, genuine work — is showing his faith by his works, and is doing, moreover, what will be sure to react to increase his faith.

But over and above this each ought to have some one thing at least, some one thing, it may be, which

will involve self-denial, thought, watchfulness, sacrifice, which is done purely for Christ. When a
man is able to say: "I do this not because it is
my inclination, nor because I think I can do it better than anybody else — whether it be teaching in
the Sunday-school, or giving money, or visiting the
sick, or helping the needy and the tempted, or leading in prayer in the social meeting, or whatever else
it may be — but I do it for Christ's sake, and to bring
those for whom He died into sympathy with Him,"
it is an assurance to his own soul that he is fully in
earnest, and that he is not deceiving himself by being
a hearer only, and not a doer of the Word.

My prescription for those whose faith is weak, or
whose faith is waning, possibly, and whose grasp,
therefore, on the things of God is feeble, and whose
religion is without any element of satisfaction or
comfort in it, is — go to work. It is not reading, it
is not meditation, it is not taking in through the ear,
it is not even prayer altogether, which will straighten
out one's ideas and bring God nearer to the soul,
but doing something — doing something in the spirit
and for the ends of the Divine Lord. Keep the brain
busy, keep the heart busy, keep the hands busy, in
the service of Him who went about doing good and
who died for us, and there will be both robustness
and joy in one's faith.

Both, then, are what we want. We want faith
and we want works. We want a faith which works by
love; and we want works which have in them the

inspiration of faith, and are the outcome of faith. Not one alone. Not one over against the other, but both — faith and works.

Let us not forget that we are living at an hour and in circumstances in which the demand is imperative for things to be done. When we think of how much there is to be done in our city; in all the great cities of the land; in our nation; in the world; how much is to be done for particular classes, for children, for drunkards, for gamblers, for populations which know nothing and care nothing for our Gospel of Jesus Christ, it seems appalling; and there is a temptation to sit down and fold the hands and do nothing. For what will the little which one person can do amount to against this great bulk of work which cries out to be done? But each standing in his own place and lot, each doing what he can day by day, in the cause and for the interest of the kingdom, in God's own time will solve the problem of the world's conversion to the faith of the Son of God, and the turning over of the nations of the earth to our Lord and His Christ.

A DIFFERENCE BETWEEN THEM.

But all the children of Israel had light in their dwellings.
Exodus 10: 23.

WHATEVER may be thought of the spirit and method and wisdom and taste of some of the more earnest of the evangelists who appear before our churches from time to time, and whatever may be the outcome of their labors, they are certainly right in the sharp emphasis they lay on the difference which ought to exist between the children of God and the children of the world.

It is not the same thing to be in the church and to be out of the church. It is not the same thing to live a life of faith on the Son of God, and a life which is molded on the policies of a time-serving generation and the customs and fashions of a pleasure-seeking society. The word of Jesus is: "Ye cannot serve God and Mammon." The word of the Apostle is: "Be not conformed to this world, but be ye transformed." The word of still another Apostle is: "Love not the world, neither the things that are in the world. If any man love the world, the love of the Father is not in him. For all that is in the world, the lust of the flesh and the lust of the eyes and the vain

149

glory of life, is not of the Father, but is of the world."
"Come out from among them, and be ye separate,"
saith the Lord. "Holy, harmless, undefiled, separate from sinners" is the description of Him whom
we are to follow, and whom we are to be like.

It is right to say these things and to insist upon
them. Whoever says them utters the truth. It is
not seemly that a man's membership in the church
should be known only through the published lists of
the manual. It is not seemly that a disciple of Jesus
Christ should be just as well up in horse-racing and
theater-going and card-playing and all the gaieties
and frivolities of the ball-room as the most accomplished worldling. It is not according to any New
Testament conception of home relations and home
responsibilities that a Christian husband and father
should leave his wife and children and wander off to
spend his evenings amid the elegant dissipations of
the club. Among the dread revelations of the world
to come will be some of the temptations yielded to,
and some of the bad lessons learned, and some of
the experiences registered, within the retreats of
these popular clubs. It is nothing short of a mon-
strous perversion of the whole idea of denying one's
self, and taking up one's cross, and following Jesus,
to make public confession of faith in the Divine Redeemer, and then to go right on, living in the realm
of the appetites and the passions and the senses,
pursuing business and politics and pleasure, after
precisely the same methods and with the same ab-

sorbing eagerness, of men who deliberately put away from their minds all thought of the future and live on from day to day without God and without hope. It may be scouted as a Puritan notion — narrow, bigoted and without a place in the broader and freer views of this liberal age; but a life, to fall in at all with the Bible ideal, will be other than an ordinary worldly life. It will be conspicuous, not alone for the creed to which assent is given and the warmth of its holy enthusiasm, but for the elevation of its sentiments and the purity of its thoughts and aims. So far from superseding the high and exacting standards of other days, the advancement of the present time underscores the obligation to be clean and straightforward and everywhere and always exemplary. There never was a time when gross, selfish living, when drinking and gambling, and lying and cheating, and taking advantage of technicalities in bargains and laws to overreach men in business transactions, were more mischievous than now, and when the evil influences of such proceedings would be likely to reach farther. It is bad in anybody; it is harmful in anybody; but when a man who is known to have avowed his faith in Christ is mean and morally crooked, and full of all sorts of schemes for evading his own responsibilities and getting the better of other people, it is a recreancy to be rebuked right and left. There is too much of this. The instances are too many in which church-members are constantly taxing their associates to exercise the charity which covers a multitude of sins.

Even where there are no flagrant transgressions, there is a secular temper which weakens faith, and chills love, and abates zeal. There is no use in denying it, the church is crippled and compromised by the worldly spirit which pervades it. While the few are earnest, devoted, self-sacrificing, conscientious in ascertaining and observing God's will, studious of ways and methods in which they can project their energy forward along lines of Christian activity, and spend and be spent in the service of the kingdom, the many are at ease, going at the same gait at which the world goes, speaking in the same accents of indifference and selfishness with which the world speaks, and finding the law of their life, not in the open Word of God, not in the example of Jesus Christ, not in the pleading needs of humanity, but in their own inclinations and love of indulgence and the average conduct of well-to-do people about them.

We may quarrel with men who tell us these things, and say they are impertinent, coarse, vulgar, or even go so far as to lodge against them the crowning demerit of being ungrammatical, but they are good wholesome things to be told to us. We better listen. Better smash in the doors, and haul men and women and children out of their beds quite unceremoniously than to wait for introductions and all the forms of etiquette when the house is on fire. There are a plenty of men who are prophesying smooth things to us in faultless diction. If there is anybody to come and tell us God's truth, let us receive it, though it be clothed in the homely garb of bluntest speech. When men are riding straight down to perdition in the gilded chariots of culture and mutual admiration, it can do no harm to jolt the wheels just a little with a few cobble stones of plain Anglo-Saxon. We tolerate nakedness in the theater; we fairly dote over the nude in art; and if a man does not blush at some of the exhibitions which are made at what are called, with fine irony, "full dress" parties, it is because his native modesty has been laid in sacrifice on the altar of custom; let us not squirm if, now and then, we are treated to *the naked truth!*

The misfortune is that we are more sensitive on the side of æsthetics than we are on the side of morals. Things abhorrent to God and man and all decency, are done, and we are not over-much shocked; but whoever tells the story, does it at infinite risk. There is likely to be ten times as much indignation and protest against the indelicacy of the story as against the measureless iniquity lying behind the story.

The early experience of Parkhurst was not extraordinary. It is a common thing to pick flaws in men and to hamper them with criticisms, if we do not happen to like the things they bring us. If our fond dreams are disturbed; if our pride is wounded; if our little formulas of propriety are ignored; if our sensibilities are offended; if our ease is broken in upon and our interests are in any way invaded, then there is trouble at once.

Elijah went to Ahab with a message from God;
straightway there was an assault on the messenger,
and he had to flee for his life.   Isaiah did not mince
matters as he charged home their crimes and delinquencies upon the people.   "Ah, sinful nation, a
people laden with iniquity."   "From the sole of the
foot even unto the head, no soundness."   "How is
the faithful city become an harlot!"   "Full of murderers;" "silver debased into dross;" "wine mixed
with water;" "the princes in rebellion and companion-
ing with thieves;" "bribery everywhere;" "fatherless
children and widows wronged without compunction."
The tradition is that they sawed him asunder.
From Josiah to the captivity, Jerusalem swarmed
with easy-going prophets, who said it was all a
mistake about the wrath of God being kindled against
them, and punishments impending over them; but
Jeremiah went right on telling the truth, thrusting
the probe to the very core of the national soreness,
and reiterating in angered ears that there was nothing
short of seventy years of exile and bondage and oppression for their gross idolatry and corruption; and
they repaid him with slander and imprisonment and
every abuse.   John the Baptist ventured to talk very
plainly — and to be very personal in his talk — about
adultery committed by parties in high station. Mrs.
Herod's delicate and sensitive soul was offended, and
the result was that the head of this faithful preacher
of righteousness was borne to her on a charger.
Paul was master of no art — scholar and logician and

rhetorician as he was — by which he could tell the truth to men, and at the same time not madden large numbers of them. Plain-speaking — dissatisfaction, opposition, assaults one after another, arrests, expulsion from this place and that, final martyrdom — that is the story in outline on the secular side of the apostles' ministry.

Even the Great Teacher was never able to lay bare the self-conceit and the pride and the worldliness and the extortions and the corruptions of people who considered themselves respectable, without immediate peril to peace and life. Poor, miserable sinners — men and women who were conscious there was nothing in them but moral rottenness — were glad in his searching words, for they wanted to see themselves as God saw them, and to know their needs, and to be helped; and they had sense enough to understand there was no help for them but in utmost openness and sincerity. But when He laid the scourge on the backs of men who were in good and regular standing in the church, and who moved in the best circles, and who helped set the fashions in dress and equipage and amusements and benevolence and all that, there was wincing, and growling, and gnashing of teeth, and more than once there had to be a hurried escape from violent hands.

No. Men who have had messages from God to a gay and adulterous generation, and whose souls have been on fire with the purpose to lift the church out of formalism and worldliness and turn hearts anew to faith and love and righteousness, have never had an easy time of it. If it has not been one objection, it has been another. They said of Martin Luther that he was vulgar and over-plain of speech. The question was not: "Are his charges true?" but: "Are they preferred with sufficient refinement of language?" They said of John Knox that he was coarse, and that his rudeness in speaking of the dignitaries of church and state ought to be checked and punished. The holy horror was felt not at the wrongs which were inflicted on the people by the heartless authorities, but at the manner in which these wrongs were assailed. It was going to bring religion into reproach, and hinder the cause. They said of John Wesley that he was ambitious and heady. Had John Wesley taken counsel of other people's fears and other people's tastes, there would have been no Methodist church in the world to-day.

Here the main point of the whole business — which is that there is meant to be a difference, and ought to be a difference, and will be a difference if believers are true to their Lord and true to themselves, between the people of God and the people of the world — opens out to us once more. On this there are two thoughts to be pressed:

The first one is that God is trying, and through all the ages of the church has been trying, to make it evident to all eyes that men who avow their faith in Him, and claim to be walking in His fellowship and to be aiming to do His will, are to be unlike —

unlike in the habit and temper with which they conduct secular affairs, and eminently unlike in their
moral and spiritual superiority — to the unbelieving
and indifferent masses about them. "Be ye holy,
for I am holy."

In the old version the people of God are called *a
peculiar people.* "But ye are a chosen generation,
a royal priesthood, an holy nation, a peculiar people."
It is an old familiar witticism to say, it must be admitted that some of them are "peculiar" — very
"peculiar." But the new version removes all possibility of a double significance and the play of sar-
casm by translating the phrase as *a people for God's
own possession.* That is what "peculiar" means,
and that is what the "peculiar" is to consist in — *being God's own.* In all their powers and faculties,
in all their culture and substance, in all the possibilities of their being, the people of God are to be
God's own.

Sentences from the sacred Scriptures already
quoted make this more than manifest. God is never
weary of emphasizing the unlikeness, as it exists in
His mind and aim, between men who are of the
earth, earthy, and men who are taken up with
heavenly vocations. In multitudinous precepts,
running all the way from Genesis to Revelation;
through the exalted standards held up by a long line
of prophets and apostles and the protests which fell
from their lips against all sorts of iniquity; through
the ministry of the Spirit, guiding into the truth, en-

forcing duty, rebuking for sin and unrighteousness, and girding with strength so that one shall be equal to burden-bearing and to sharp moral conflicts; in the history of the church, which has been invincible, aggressive, victorious always when it has been firm in its grasp on faith and simple and correct and pure in its walk before the world, and which has invariably suffered defeat and been forced down into the valley of humiliation whenever it has come under the power of material policies and ambitions; and in providences, too, in which He has shown the tokens of His favor to those who were His own, and has set the marks of His disapprobation on the impure and the disobedient and the scheming and selfish — God has said: "My people must be unlike the people of the world."

That is a very significant and instructive fact which our text recites concerning the children of Israel down in Goshen. "But all the children of Israel had light in their dwellings." Nobody else had light; but the children of Israel had it.

Back at the fourth plague God had made promise of His special interposition in behalf of the oppressed Israelites. "And I will sever in that day the land of Goshen, in which my people dwell, that no swarms of flies shall be there; to the end that thou mayest know that I am the Lord in the midst of thee. And I will put a division between my people and thy people." This was what the Lord instructed Moses to say to the obstinate and obdurate ruler of the Egyptians.

Consequently, when the threatened *swarm of flies* came, and the house of Pharaoh was filled, and the houses of the servants were filled, and there were inconvenience and annoyance everywhere, the children of Israel were unmolested. There was "a division" between the people of God and the people of Pharaoh.

When the swarm of flies was followed by the plague of *a very grievous murrain,* and the horses and the asses and the camels and the oxen and the sheep of Egypt were attacked with the fatal malady, there was again "a division" between them, and "of the cattle of the children of Israel died not one." God set His protecting mark even upon the cattle of the children of Israel.

It was the same thing again when the awful *storm of lightning and thunder and hail* broke over the land, and fire ran along the ground, and the heavens raged and rained down their torrents of quick destruction, and men and beasts were smitten, and trees were overturned and broken, and herbs were swept away from the fields, and it was terror and wasting all up and down. There was "a division" between the people of God and the people of Pharaoh. "Only in the land of Goshen, where the children of Israel were, was there no hail." There was a moral purpose in the storm; and sleet and hail and wind and flashing lightning swept along the path, and made the circuit God had appointed. Awful storm smiting the Egyptians, but out there in the land of Goshen, among the children of Israel, all was calm and quiet as a summer morning.

Further on there came the plague of *the thick darkness* — even of "a darkness that might be felt." "And Moses stretched forth his hand toward heaven; and there was a thick darkness in all the land of Egypt three days. They saw not one another, neither rose any from their place, for three days." As the Author of the Book of Wisdom says: "They were not only prisoners of darkness and fettered with the bonds of a long night; but they were horribly astonished likewise, and troubled with strange apparitions." *But all the children of Israel had light in their dwellings.* There was sunshine in Goshen. No man was hindered in his labor. Each could rise as usual; each could come and go at his pleasure; and the sun and moon and stars rendered their wonted service. It was to the Egyptians alone that there came the terrible and awful pre-intimation of the blackness of darkness which is the fit expression and fit reward of deliberate sin. Not always, not often in such a signal way as this does the warning come, but sooner or later sin enshrouds in darkness, and men's perceptions become clouded and they can not see. There is, perhaps, hardly another emblem better suited to express God's thought of sin and to foreshadow what will be the final consequences of sin, than this deep darkness of Egypt, which for three days held the people in the depths and gloom of night.

But there was sunshine in Goshen. God gave to the children of Israel that token of His care and of His intent to lead them out from their bondage and oppression and sorrows and tears. He made it as evident as light is from darkness, by His special and eminent regard for his own, that there was a difference between the children of Israel and the children of Pharaoh.

It has been conjectured that it was with reference to this fact in the history of the chosen people, and the "division" made between them and their enemies, that the prophet broke out in the words: "Arise, shine, for thy light is come, and the glory of the Lord is risen upon thee. For behold, darkness shall cover the earth, and gross darkness the people; but the Lord shall *rise upon thee*, and His glory shall *be seen upon thee*." God was to come to them with His light, and they were to know it, and to have share in it through a blessed inward experience; and it was all to be so clear and conspicuous that others could not help witnessing it. "And His glory *shall be seen upon thee*."

It is a firm conviction of mine that God's people are never without these signs and tokens of His gracious will. If it is not always made evident to the world, it is made evident to them and they know it by a thousand unmistakable indications, that in inducing them to accept His love and come into His fellowship and service, He means for them a clean, unworldly life. One cannot love the things God loves, and walk in His ways, without inward propulsion in this direction.

When men, therefore, insist sharply on purity, on unworldliness, on a clear and unmistakable unlikeness on the part of the disciples of Jesus to those who care nothing for His message and His character, and on avoiding the very appearance of evil, they aie in the exact line of God's thought. When men go to the bottom, and call things by their right names, and deal unsparingly with iniquity and pet sins and hollow pretense of piety and limp acquiescences in schemes in which "good Lord" and "good devil" are mingled in about equal proportions, even though it be done in language which would put to flight the rules of Lindley Murray, and shock a modern drawing-room, they are still in the line of the apostolic succession, and their rebukes of the shortcomings and the transgressions and the shameless profligacies of those who pretend to be the children of God here upon the earth and heirs of the everlasting inheritance, awake — so we feel sure — echoes of approval in all the heavenly hosts. When there is no more sinning in the church, and there is no more ugly compromising of Christian character, and men who have named the name of Christ are strict to depart from iniquity, and the things of time and sense have lost their consuming fascination for those who confess themselves to be pilgrims and strangers in the earth, rebukes will be out of order, and we may insist on the prophesying of smooth things. But that time is not yet.

The second thought on which stress is laid is that as God emphasizes the difference which exists in theory and which ought to exist in practice between His own people and the people of the world, and is all the time trying to make this difference just as wide as possible by getting His people into an ever increasing nearness and likeness to Him, so it should be the distinct endeavor of all who claim to be walking by faith and not by sight, and who expect to find the enduring satisfactions and rewards of life not here in this shadow-realm, but yonder in the city which hath foundations, to co-work with God, and press forward into a separateness from sinners which shall be pronounced and unmistakable.

It goes without saying, of course, that the suggestion here urged looks to something quite other than a mere Pharisaic formalism and scrupulousness. A man who is unlike other men only in the boastful tone of his prayers and in the breadth of his phylacteries and in his observance of the letter which killeth and in the thought of his own surpassing piety, better not be so much unlike them. The conceit of holiness is one of the worst forms of unholiness.

But the difference which is emphasized by the fact that one sincerely loves God and delights in communion with Him; that one has the reverent fear through which the secret of the Lord is whispered to the soul; that one finds light and joy in the Word and in the observance of the Sabbath and in the great congregation gathered for service in the house of worship

and in the fellowship of the "two or three" who
come together in the Lord's name to talk with Him
and with each other about the things of soul; that
one will not lie, nor cheat, nor steal, nor meanly
equivocate, nor slander, nor shirk; that one will not
permit associations, nor fall into courses of conduct, nor take up any forms of self-indulgence and
self-gratification and self-seeking, whose tendencies
are to arrest his own spiritual development and to
hinder the growth of the kingdom which is not meat
and drink, but righteousness and peace and joy in
the Holy Ghost; that one is disposed to be helpful
according to the utmost measure of ability in supply-
ing needs, in drying tears, in soothing sorrows, in
restoring the wayward and sinful, and bringing all
humanity into loving accord with the Divine Father
— of this difference let us have more and more till
the reign of righteousness is universal, and the kingdoms of the earth have become the kingdoms of our
Lord and His Christ. If only the difference which
ought to exist along these lines could be actualized
here in Chicago, the mighty power of the church
would be felt once more as in the old Pentecostal
times, and the whole face of things would be changed
in a month.

It were a happy thing were the moral standards
of the world so far advanced as to obviate the necessity of any wide difference between believers and unbelievers. Unfortunately this is not the case. In
many particulars there has been marked progress.

In many particulars the outlook is full of encourage-
ment. But the world is still the world, and flesh
and devil are still flesh and devil. It ought, therefore, to startle a man who is nominally a Christian
man, as though there were in it a fore-gleam of the
judgment, to discover that there is no sharp line running through and marking off his life, in the inner
thought and spirit of it, in the general tone and conduct of it and in the sweep of its influences, from
the lives of those who have never made any effort
to come into conscious affiliation with God. If a man
has no more faith than those who frankly admit that
they are faithless; no more love; no more consecration; no more identification with the great and
pressing enterprises of the church, — on what ground
shall he make it appear to himself that he is a child
of God? No man ought to be content with minimum
attainments — with attainments, that is, which will
just barely put him on the side of the people of the
Lord; but he ought to push for the highest acqui-
sitions of knowledge and grace and spiritual force.
"If so be that I may apprehend that for which also
I was apprehended by Christ Jesus" was the noble
aspiration of the great Apostle.

When believers have apprehended that for which
they have been apprehended by their Divine Lord,
there will be no longer any difficulty in distinguish-
ing between them and unbelievers. It will be in their
speech; it will be in their plans; it will be in the
prevailing temper of their minds; it will be in the at-

mosphere of their homes and stores and mills and shops; it will be in the attitudes they will assume face to face with disappointment and under afflictions. Every day's experience will seem to make this difference more marked and manifest. Others beholding them will say: "These are men whose hands are clean; whose faces burn with light from the face of God; who walk in faith; who are rooted and grounded in love; who are strengthened with might by the Spirit in the inner man, and who aspire to be filled with all the fullness of God."

There is a suggestive and pertinent passage in the Epistle of Paul to Titus, and with that these words may fitly close: *For the grace of God hath appeared, bringing salvation unto all men, instructing us to the intent that, denying ungodliness and worldly lusts, we should live soberly and righteously and godly in this present world; looking for the blessed hope and appearing of the glory of our great God and Saviour Jesus Christ, who gave himself for us, that He might redeem us from all iniquity, and purify unto Himself a people for his own possession, zealous of good works.*

THE RECEPTIVE MIND.

For indeed we have had good tidings preached unto us, even as also they have; but the word of hearing did not profit them, because they were not united by faith with them that heard. Heb. 4: 2.

RUSKIN has said that no man is competent to judge of the merits of a picture who looks only at its faults. The thought contained in the statement is capable of infinite applications. No man is in a mood to receive good from a truth, no matter of what sort nor in what form presented, whose mind is filled with prejudices against it, or who is even indifferent to its alleged claims. Ideas, like guests, to be most companionable and to yield best results, must be met with generous hospitality.

In line with this thought our present theme is to be: *The Receptive Mind.*

This was the difficulty in the instance under review. There was a lack of the receptive mind. There was no openness to divine disclosures; no eager and responsive interest in facts declared; no hearty sympathy with promises made. On the contrary, all the avenues of spiritual approach were practically sealed against God. There was the light; but the eye was shut. There was the voice, calling, ready to guide, ready to comfort, full of all sweetness; but the ear was stopped. There was the rest, promised,

assured; but there was no heart for it and no genuine belief in its reality and value. There was an
evil heart of unbelief through which they were led
to depart from the living God, and to put all the
tender, wise words He addressed to them, and all the
helpful influences He poured in upon their lives, deliberately behind them.

The point pressed by the inspired writer is that
this very grave and fatal mistake may be repeated.
"Take heed, brethren, lest haply there shall be in
any one of you an evil heart of unbelief . . . for
we are become partakers of Christ, if we hold fast
the beginning of our confidence, firm unto the end."
It was because they believed not that God was grieved
with the children of Israel; and it was because
they believed not that they were not permitted to
enter into the rest of the Promised Land. A rest
was promised; but it was of no advantage to them, —
so far as they were concerned might just as well not
have been promised — because it was not met with a
response of faith. This is the secret of the failure.
There was no temper of receptivity, — no downright
and sincere eagerness to know if the things declared
were true or not, — nothing but hard, repellent unbelief for God's promises to strike against.

This is where we are to have a care. The old
peril is the new peril. In every generation men are
falling after the same example of unbelief. The forgiveness awaits; the promises abide; the invitation,
tender, urgent, still is — "come;" and help and guid-

ance and abundant rewards are assured; but through lack of the receptive mind multitudes miss entering in and enjoying what God has in store for them.

Now this unbelief, or lack of faith, which the author of our text deprecates and rebukes, takes three practical forms, each of which is likely to be fatal.

I. *It takes the form of studied indifference to all religious truths and claims.*

Men affirm that they have no interest in these questions. It is not merely that they are preoccupied with other things, — with studies which engross their minds, with business matters, with pleasures, with politics and what not; but they feel no drawings, so they tell us, and no stress of necessity to grapple with spiritual problems. When pressed they refuse to admit any obligation to meet the issue of God and their own souls. Anything else whose advocates should claim for it commanding importance, they would consider and investigate according to ability; but not religion. Many of these people pride themselves on their fairness and candor. They are conscientious in weighing both sides of matters submitted to them until it comes to Christianity, and then they bar the doors, and, on the ground that they care for none of these things, decline to give those who would persuade them into the faith of the Son of God an open chance to do their work.

But is this a sound position? Has any man a moral right to be indifferent to the truths and claims of the

Christian religion? Can a man pass by on the other side of Jesus and be guiltless?

Bear these two or three things in mind. Religion goes to the heart of our personality, and has to do with our inmost being. It concerns origin and destiny, whence we came and whither we go. In the finest conception and in the utmost reaches of them, it concerns life and law and duty. All the momentous questions of the here and the hereafter are wrapped up in the folds of religion. To blot stars out of the firmament would not be of so much consequence as to blot thought of religion out of the sky of the soul. No man has been true to himself, and met properly the grave responsibilities which rest upon him in virtue of his rational existence, until he has come to some sort of thorough and honest conclusion about God. True or false, this is what religion is — one of the most potent factors in the shaping of laws and customs and in the development of civilization. May a man be indifferent to it?

A man may say if he will, that he is not interested in historical researches; in explorations, Egyptian, Babylonian, African, Asiatic; in inventions like those of Bessemer and Bell and Edison; in the platforms of parties and the rivalries and conquests of ruling dynasties; in the details of scientific investigations; in social questions and reforms — though it is hard to see how one can be a man and hold his place in an active, progressive community, and not have his thoughts and sympathies drawn out in some of these

directions; but to say that the things which touch
the soul in its inmost core and in its highest relations
are of no concern to him — that he puts them by as
he would the idle wind — would seem to be a kind of
abdication of the supreme and most sacred functions
of the rational faculties.

As has just been intimated, these questions of religion come to one in the very structure of his soul.
They are interwoven with all the facts and orders
and methods of nature. The man of science may
say: "I will have nothing to do with theories and
problems of theology; I will study astronomy, and
stop there; or geology, and stop there; or botany,
and stop there; or anatomy, and stop there; or
metaphysics, and stop there;" but no, he cannot
stop there. Every atom is more than an atom; it is
a question. Every lily is more than a lily; it is a
question. Every star is more than a star; it is a
question. Every instinct is more than an instinct; it
is a question. Every thought is more than a thought;
it is a question. Heaven and earth and all life are
punctuated with interrogation points. The suggestion
of God is everywhere forced upon us. We may stop
our ears and refuse to listen; but from realms unseen
the question will keep coming. Every bush is aflame
with challenges to stop and think what we are and
where we are and what our duty and destiny.

II. *This unbelief, or lack of faith, takes the further form of positive opposition to religious truths
and claims.*

It becomes belligerent and noisy. It lifts up its voice in the streets. It mounts platforms. It writes books. It edits newspapers. It founds magazines. It circulates tracts. It organizes societies. It seeks and makes proselytes of all whom it can influence. If it finds men bending down before the Most High in the reverent attitude of prayer, it tries, sometimes by argument and sometimes by ridicule, to divert their minds and draw them away from the sacred and blessed service. If it encounters men who are clear and strong in their conviction of the immortality of the soul and the fatherhood of God and the saving power of Christ and the blessedness of believers in the world to come, with a cunning and malignity which it would seem harsh fitly to characterize, it undertakes to sift their minds full of the fine dust of doubt, and to choke the inlets of divine light, and to arrest the flow of sweet spiritual joy in their lives. It is never so jubilant, — this positive, aggressive unbelief, as when it can succeed in silencing some preacher's voice, or perchance transferring some erratic minister from what he is pleased to call the cramped arena of the pulpit to the broader domain of the boards of a theater.

Proceeding under the guise of benevolence, it claims that to rob men of their faith in God is to enrich humanity. It mocks and deplores Sabbath-schools and all kinds of schools for Bible-instruction, because these schools fill the minds of the young with preconceived ideas of God, and so give them notions of faith and love and purity and duty hard to eradicate.

This form of unbelief does its best to seal all eyes against heavenly visions, to close all ears against still small voices, to render spiritual nerves insensible to the healing and guiding touch of the Divine hand, and to reduce the race to a condition of hopeless orphanage.

Every name of weight which stands for opposition to Christianity; every apparent difficulty and inconsistency in revelation; every folly and wickedness committed by men inside the church and under the name of religion; every seeming cross-purpose discoverable in the working out of the ends of God in providence; everything hard to be understood and hard to be reconciled with unerring wisdom and infinite love, is called up; and then all these are set in array together, and the question is asked, sometimes in a half pitiful tone, sometimes in a sneering tone, but always in a tone to imply that only one answer can be given in face of such facts and so many of them, whether men of intelligence and breadth of view and courage of conviction are to be expected to hold fast the old faith in the supernatural, and to live and die in the confidence that there is a personal God, a Divine Father and Helper, who is not far from each one of us.

There are men who disbelieve, who are yet quiet in their unbelief. They are honest doubters, and it pains them that they cannot see their way clearly in these matters of the soul and God. But the unbelievers now in mind are active, determined. Like Saul of Tarsus, they are exceeding mad against the faith and all who hold it. They stick at nothing which has promise in it of overturning the trust of disciples in their Lord. They shut God out from their own souls, and they do the best they can to shut Him out of all souls.

III. *This unbelief, or lack of faith, has its explanation and takes form also in courses of conduct which are in direct contravention of the truths and claims of religion, and which make the approaches of light both difficult and unwelcome.*

It is the unbelief of bad action. It is the dissent of dishonesty and immorality and a low, gross earthiness. It is the opposition of unworthy character. It is the attitude men take when they permit themselves to be dominated by their passions and their appetites and their mean greeds, rather than by reason and conscience and a will which is loyal to virtue. They refuse to believe God, — refuse, indeed, to believe there is any God, because such belief would seriously interfere with their malicious designs or the pleasure they find in their sensual indulgences. Faith in God would obstruct and disturb them in their evil ways.

This is exactly as the Psalmist sets it forth: "The transgression of the wicked saith within my heart that there is no fear of God before his eyes." He has put God and the fear of God away from his thought because with God and the fear of God in mind he cannot go on with his wickedness. It is so with all evil-doers. God wants purity; they prefer to be impure. God wants veracity; they stick at no lies. God wants unselfishness, generosity, a spirit of helpfulness to run from man to man and bless the world; they are hard, oppressive, extortionate, so that the faces of the poor grow thinner and thinner under their cruel grinding;— or they are gluttons and wine-bibbers and revolting sensualists. God wants acknowledgment, reverence, obedience, love; they turn away from Him and His demands as though He were an obtrusive and impertinent beggar, asking for that to which He has no right.

Now is it not evident that unbelief, taking either of these forms, must necessarily obstruct the inflow of God's blessing on the soul? "He that cometh to God must believe that He is, and that He is a rewarder of them who diligently seek Him." So, too, he to whom God comes must believe that He is, and that His presence in love is the supreme benediction.

If, to retrace our steps a little, men are indifferent to God, refuse to think about Him, refuse to consider the ground on which He makes His appeals to their reason and conscience, but persistently preoccupy and fill their minds with other things, how can they be helped? Flood a room with light, hang all its walls with rarest pictures — but if men will not open their eyes to them — say they care nothing about them — what good will it do? Raphael and Rembrandt and Titian and Reynolds might as well never have painted. Fill the air with music of quiring angels; pour out instruction, volume on volume, hot and luminous as eloquent lips can make it; and yet if men will not take pains to listen, say they have no interest in listening, and in this temper turn their ears away to be filled with other sounds, how are they to be edified by it all? There might as well have been no Handel or Mozart to sing and no Demosthenes or Wendell Phillips to speak. There must be open-mindedness as opposed to indifference.

If men go further, and become out-and-out obstructionists, fighters against God and faith in God, do they not violate all the conditions on which light might be expected to find its way into their souls? Do they not violate all the conditions, indeed, on which light ever does find its way into the soul? Drawing near to God brings God near to us. Drawing outward from God widens the space, always too wide, alas! between Him and us.

Doubt, as has already been implied, is not altogether abnormal, still less altogether criminal. There is much doubt that is genuine and sincere, and even praiseworthy. Employed as a spur to honest investigation, doubt is good. Treated as the tools with which to plow and harrow and cultivate the soil, and not as the crop which is the final outcome of all the labor, doubt may be fruitful of rich spiritual harvests. But doubt petted, doubt made a ground of pride as though it were proof of superior intellectual keenness and breadth, doubt nourished and developed until it clouds all the sky where the stars of hope shine, and God comes no longer within the horizon of the soul's vision, and one is tempted to exclaim with the fool, "There is no God,"— is a sore calamity. This kind of doubt is more than likely to become conceited, obtrusive, offensive, and to end in a spiritual mood which it does no violence to language to call "enmity against God."

Enmity, it is easy to see, draws the curtain against light. Enmity fills the soul with prejudice, and arms it with weapons of opposition. To continue in a mood of enmity against God and His truth and His law and His institutions, disloyal, oppugnant, is to put out of the question all chances of receiving good from His Gospel, or from the influences He lavishes upon us, and with which He seeks to restrain and guide us.

If men, again, are intent on iniquity — steeped in corruption — and are unwilling to break off their sins by righteousness, simply hearing the word will bring no blessing to them. They hear; but they go right on. They see; but they pause not, and sin is still rolled as a sweet morsel under their tongues. There is light for them; but they love darkness rather than light, because their deeds are evil. There is a shining way open to their feet; but they go plunging down from depth to depth — from deep to deeper deep — in a night of ever thickening gloom. Salvation may be pressed upon them; they prefer to remain without

hope and without God in the world. Heaven with
all its wealth of glory may be laid before them; they
choose rather to enjoy the pleasures of sin for a sea-
son. Their knowledge, their opportunities do not
profit them, because their hearts and their lives are
full of evil deeds.

What then is wanted?

In general, an open, receptive mind; a mind, that
is, which discards all prejudices, and welcomes truth
under whatever garb and wherever found, just as
the earth welcomes the dawning of the day.

Specifically these three things:

I.   *The same gracious candor in considering religious truths and claims one carries, and ought to
carry, into the consideration of the facts and laws
and methods of science.*

Why not? If a man is to derive any good from the
study of Aristotle or Darwin or Huxley or Spencer or Lubbock or Agassiz, he must approach his
author in the spirit of docility which consents to believe there may be some justification for the inferences he draws and the system he builds up. The
man who says of Plato there is nothing in him and
he is not worth reading, will be likely to find nothing
in him.

What is asked, and all that is asked now, is that
a man will read the Word of God in the same generous temper in which he wishes others to read the
"Origin of Species" or "Pre-Historic Man." Is this
done? Do men, and especially a certain class of

men, canvass religious questions and weigh the arguments for the existence of a divine being — personal and supreme — and for the spirituality and immortality of the soul and for the sonship and saving power of Jesus Christ and for all the truths of the Christian Faith just as carefully and honestly as they expect, and have a right to expect others to go over the ground of "Evolution" or "The Correlation of Forces" or "Social Ethics"? Is it not true that thousands and thousands of intelligent people set religion aside without ever devoting a single day to the earnest consideration of the subject? They yield to prejudice and dismiss it without examination.

2. *There is wanted the admission of the presumption that religious truths have not been held, and religious claims acknowledged, by so many men throughout the ages without some basis in reason.*

It is asserted that there has been great progress in the world since the beginning of things, and particularly during these latest years.

This is true. We travel with more facility. One may lunch on Thursday at Queenstown, and on the next Thursday be dining at home with his family in Chicago. We fight with more deadly weapons. What would Macedonian phalanxes under Alexander or Valley Forge patriots under Washington have been able to do with Krupp guns? We can send and receive tidings quicker. It takes the laggard hands on the dial of an Illinois clock six hours to catch up with the date of the news already before us that the Duke of Clarence or Manning or Spurgeon is dead. We have vastly better machinery for sowing and reaping. No doubt even the faithful Ruth would have stopped her gleaning in sheer wonder had she seen a McCormick reaper suddenly descend and go moving back and forth in the field of Boaz. We spin and weave with a speed and ingenuity never dreamed of even so late as a hundred years ago. Imagine Penelope, the faithful spouse of the wandering Ulysses, or Priscilla, the sweet Puritan maiden who did not marry Captain Miles Standish, standing in presence of a Nottingham lace-machine, or an Axminster loom! We live in more comfortable homes. We have books and magazines and newspapers till they are an incumbrance. The improvements along material lines and the wider grasp on many of the facts of nature which characterize our day cannot be questioned. The advance, too, has been for the most part beneficent. The masses have shared in the immense benefits of this advance, and life means more and is more to the millions than it otherwise could have been.

But how about the human faculties themselves? How about the senses, the reason, the conscience? Has the capacity to see and to know and to understand made such forward strides that the keenest and profoundest intellects of the olden times were as puny children in comparison with what the keenest and profoundest intellects have come to be now?

Take it in the sphere of moral duties and moral ob-

ligations. Have we risen to anything better than
Moses knew and experienced in the Ten Commandments? Were men to keep these Commandments,
as our Lord interpreted them, God would get His
due, and not a human being in all the earth would
ever again be wronged.

Take it in the sphere of pure thought. Has the
genius of man ever produced anything grander than
the book of Job? Turn to Carlyle in his "Hero-Wor-
ship," and see what he thinks of it. "I call that,"
so he says, "apart from all theories about it, one of
the grandest things ever written with pen. . . .
A noble book; all men's book. It is our first, oldest
statement of the never-ending problem;—man's
destiny and God's ways with him here in this earth.
And all in such free flowing outlines; grand in its
sincerity, in its simplicity, in its epic melody and
repose of reconcilement. So *true* every way; true
eyesight and vision of all things; material things no
less than spiritual. . . . Such living likenesses
were never since drawn. Sublime sorrow, sublime
reconciliation, oldest choral melody as of the heart
of mankind,—so soft and great; as the summer midnight, as the world with its seas and stars. There is
nothing written, I think, in the Bible or out of it, of
equal literary merit."

Take it in the sphere of the analysis of heart and
life and of solemn, sincere confession as in the judgment and before God. Is there any mate to the Fifty-
first Psalm? Does the "Scarlet Letter" search deeper,

and probe with a more awful instrument of contrition and pain? The plummet of the sounding line of David goes to the bottom of sorrow for sin and of sincere repentance.

Are we beyond the Sermon on the Mount? We have Bacon; we have Emerson; we have Mill; we have Spencer; we have Shakespeare and Goethe and Milton and Wordsworth, — essayists, philosophers, scientists, poets, men of resplendent abilities, all of them, and some of them of transcendent genius; but what page in the writings of any one of these would one venture to match against the Sermon on the Mount? In my judgment it will require a good deal of first-class evolution to get us beyond the heights on which Jesus stood.

Now is it not better to conclude at once that these men — even though they lived so many centuries ago — knew whereof they spoke? They were not the victims of a baseless superstition which ought long ago to have perished from the earth; nor of a mere narrow system of thought and life which more light would be sure to displace and supersede; but they had reason on their side; and they were able from first to last and in face of all objections to give a reason for the faith that was in them. Thinking, reasoning, weighing matters, looking into the heart of things are not modern inventions. The men who have been saying from of old till this hour that there is a God, and the heavens declare His glory, and the firmament showeth His handiwork, and man is His witness, have not been fools. Religion is entitled to the presumption of reasonableness.

3. *There is wanted a recognition of the responsibility each is under to investigate and settle for himself the questions of his relations to God and of his duty toward God.*

A great many seem to think all they have to do in the matter is simply to stand still and wait, like an inert, unintelligent mass, to be influenced from without. If instruction is forced upon them they will receive it, but they will not search for it as for hid treasure. If constraint is brought to bear on them till they can no longer resist it, they will yield; but not otherwise. They throw the responsibility off on God, or the servants of God.

The result is that there are multitudes who never gave the question of personal religion an hour's earnest and serious consideration in their lives. They never read the Bible; they never followed one by one the great arguments which buttress and support our Christianity; they never sought for light amongst the intelligent and devout; they never fell on their knees in prayer; they never swung wide the doors, and walked back and forth in the halls and apartments of their own souls, with a view to ascertaining whether their relations to God are what they ought to be, and whether they are in the way of realizing the true end of their being. Their attitude is that heaven must be thrust upon them, or they will not have it. They must be filled with knowledge without effort. They must be convinced against their wills. They must be taken up bodily and set over inside of salvation, or they will go on in sin. Jesus said "seek ye." Jesus said "strive." But the persons now in mind neither "seek" nor "strive;" they just wait, and drift, and let the days go by, and the years go by, and busy themselves, head and heart and hand, with everything save the one supreme concern of God and what they owe to Him.

But is this manly? Is this rational? Is this dealing wisely with our own faculties and conditions and aspirations? Is this going resolutely to the bottom of our own possible needs and perils, and laying hold with a strong hand on possible privileges which are more radiant and enduring than all the stars?

Religion is the binding of the soul to God in faith and love and loyalty. It is not a myth. It is not a superstition. It is not an empty formulary. It is not a worn-out tradition. It is life and strength and joy. Concerning any man his religion or no-religion is the most significant fact. It is the primary thing, and in one way and another determines everything else. Let a man be indifferent, if he will, to his material on-getting, and to his personal comfort and name and fame and power; but on no consideration let him put aside or ignore the truths and claims of religion. He who said "I am the way," and who over and over again uttered the sweet word "Come" in such accents of infinite tenderness that it has been as heavenly music to forlorn and distressed souls ever since, also said: "Take heed how ye hear." The most momentous of all issues is involved in the simple fact of the mind closed or the mind open. In Christ's time, as was the case before, and as has been the case since, the word preached failed to profit because the preaching of it was not met in a spirit of hospitality.

Well may we make the words of Isaiah our closing entreaty: "Incline your ear and come unto me; hear and your soul shall live; and I will make an everlasting covenant with you, even the sure mercies of David."

BAD MOTHERS.

For his mother was his counselor to do wickedly. 2 *Chron-icles 22: 3.*

It is not a pleasant service, but one for which there always seems to be occasion, to speak on the theme of "*Bad Mothers*." If there is a human being in the world who is more to be pitied than any one else, it is a child with a bad mother. It is a misfortune inexpressible to have a bad father or a bad wife or a bad husband or a bad son or daughter; but to have been ushered into life by a bad mother, and to be forced to submit through all the years of opening conscience and broadening intelligence to the molding influence of a bad mother, is the climax of untoward circumstance. One may rise superior even to this adversity, but it takes rare gifts and a large amount of moral pluck and a high measure of the grace of God to enable a person to cut loose from the vicious training, and to counter-work and overcome the demoralizing atmosphere of a bad mother. Bad as others may be, there can be little doubt that a bad mother stands unrivaled in her evil eminence.

In the story of Athaliah, as given to us in the Old Testament narrative of the careers of the reigning houses of Israel and Judah, a startling illustration is

186

furnished of a bad mother. It was a case, indeed, of a bad mother succeeding a bad mother, and of hate and cruelty and viciousness and corruption all around. For Athaliah was the daughter of Ahab and Jezebel. It was a fatal blood to have in one's veins — that of Jezebel.

Jezebel was a Phenician princess. The royal family of Tyre was remarkable at that time for its religious fanaticism and its savage temper. Jezebel was a woman who concentrated in herself the reckless and licentious habits of an oriental queen and the sternest and fiercest qualities characteristic of her race. Her name became a byword in the nation, as it has become in history; and in the estimation of the decent and good all down through the centuries it has stood for all that was mean and execrable.

The mother Jezebel reappeared in the daughter Athaliah. It was a marked and sad instance of "like mother like daughter." The wife Jezebel reappeared still again in the wife Athaliah; and what Jezebel was to Ahab in urging him on to horrible wrong and blood, Athaliah was to Jehoram, whom she had married. For, as the Scriptures ingenuously state it, "He walked in the way of the kings of Israel, as did the house of Ahab; for he had the daughter of Ahab to wife; and he did that which was evil in the sight of the Lord." Jezebel having reappeared in the daughter Athaliah, and in the wife Athaliah, reappeared also in the mother Athaliah. Her counsel, her influence, her efforts were in the same fatal line of disloyalty to God, of inhumanity to man, of mad and mischievous ambition and of every crime with which one can blacken fame. She was bent on mischief, and she used everybody and everything, and adopted every measure to accomplish her evil designs. After the great revolution by which Jehu seated himself on the throne of Samaria, she killed all the members of the royal family of Judah, with the single exception of an infant named Joash, who was destined in the providence of God and under the wise management of the high priest, Jehoiada, to displace the supplanting mother-queen. Athaliah could rend her garments in righteous indignation and grief, and cry "Treason!" "Treason!" as lustily as the purest patriot in the land when vengeance finally overtook her; but all this was nothing to her when she herself was reveling in the satisfaction of usurpation and murder.

But it is not so much for the purpose of recounting the career of a strangely cruel and vicious woman of the long ago that her name is now brought to our thought, as it is for seizing the moral which lies in the statement made in the text.

This woman was a mother, and she used the sacred relationship of a mother and the measureless influence of a mother to make her own child the servant of criminal baseness. "For his mother was his counselor to do wickedly." In her thirst for blood, in her enthusiasm of tyranny and in her determination to substitute the idolatry of her Phenician race for the worship of the true God, she did not hesitate to pervert the judgment of her son and constrain him to a course which would be sure to result in disaster. As she had wrought the ruin of her husband, Jehoram, and had made his reign so discreditable and hateful that when he was dead they refused to bury him in the sepulchers of the kings, so she wrought the ruin of her son, and made his name a standing reproach to the nation. Shrewd, scheming, exceptionally influential, this mother used the confidential relationship — a relationship which ought always to be so sacred — in which she stood to her son, and all her power of fascination, to make him a wicked ruler, unjust, immoral, false to God and false to the state.

It is a gratification to think there are not many mothers in the world who are fashioned after the type of this Athaliah mother. For it is simply impossible to believe there can be any considerable number of mothers, even among those who give little expression to a sense of their religious obligations, open to the depraved purpose intelligently and deliberately to counsel their children to do things they know to be wrong and criminal. The mother instinct, wise self-interest, the standards of civilization, to say nothing of the regulative force of moral principle, go far in most instances to restrain those who have brought immortal souls into the world from urging them on into careers of wickedness and vice.

At the same time there are mothers, quite too

many of them, in the low, immoral classes, who in
their narrower sphere are guilty of just such criminal conduct toward their children as Athaliah exhibited toward her too easily influenced son. They
not only countenance them in bad actions, but they
teach them to lie and cheat and steal and become
adepts in all arts of deception. They train them into
decoys with which more skillfully and successfully
to carry on their games of fraud. Often they deny
them suitable food and clothing, and sometimes even
distort and cripple them, in order to arrest the popular
sympathy and make unhallowed gains. Many gross
appetites and worldly lusts are fed through means
obtained in this horrible way. It is unutterably sad
that there can be such mothers. It seems a caricature,
a desecration of all that is holy, to call such creatures
mothers. Unless the number of such mothers, as
well as the number of kindred fathers, can be kept
within narrow bounds, solicitude may well be felt for
society at large.

But there are mothers, who, while they do not
purpose in their hearts to be bad mothers, and who
do not even dream that they are bad mothers, and
who are unaffectedly shocked at the picture of such
a mother as has just been drawn, take attitudes and
exert influence which are too much after the example
of Athaliah. They do not put their poisonous advice
into words. They do not openly and pointedly
counsel an excessive worldliness on the part of their
children, nor in so many words suggest indirection

and dishonesty in their method of securing gain.
But they never fail to make it clear that they are
greatly pleased at any display of business smartness,
or the skill by which people are circumvented in
bargains, or the peculiar kind of sagacity which en-
ables them, to use a phrase of the time, "to get there."
There are no close inquiries into methods and means,
and no sharp rebukes administered, if it comes out
that methods and means which have been employed
to secure success are not what they ought to have
been in uprightness.

Sitting one day at the dinner-table of a parishioner,
in one of my earlier parishes, the oldest son of the
family, a fine, strong, healthy-looking young man
of twenty or twenty-one, came bounding into the room;
and almost in the same breath in which he apologized
for being late he exclaimed in tones of triumph that
he had just had a fine streak of luck. He had been
out to buy a wedding present. He found just the
article he desired; the price of it, however, was
twenty-five dollars, and he wanted to get it for twenty.
After some higgling he decided to take it at twenty-
three; but in giving him change the dealer had made
a mistake and handed back too much, and he had got-
ten his wedding present for eighteen dollars. It was his
five dollars, which had come to him in this way, over
which the young man was jubilant. The mother was
just as glad as the boy, and thought it just as fine a
bit of good fortune. When appeal was made to me
to see what "a minister" would think of such a trans-

action, the opportunity was quickly seized to show, with as much courtesy as might be, but also with as much clearness and directness, that taking advantage of a mistake of this sort is just simply stealing.

There is a vast amount of mischief done to morals by this winking at things which are not so just as they are cunning, and which are not so helpful to character as they are thought to be to bank accounts. It is not necessary to consent to wickedness in set terms to bring about the practice of wickedness. Parents sometimes say in words to a child: "You must not;" but interpreting by tones or looks or past experiences, the child understands very well that "you must not" really means "you may." Mothers ought not to be of this sort.

It does not follow that a mother can surely hold her boy to straightforwardness, to purity, to worthy and helpful ideals, even though she does her best to keep him in fellowship with truth and duty. But a mother of whom it may be possible to say, as the Scriptures say of Athaliah in relation to her son Ahaziah: "For his mother was his counselor to do wickedly," will be almost certain to see her efforts crowned with a fatal success.

Most likely, too, a mother who just leans that way, without attempting to formulate her secret thought or her sympathy into pronounceable sentences, will have the grace of God to thank or the Divine providence or the wholesome aid of friends or a moral resoluteness much superior to what might have been expected, if her influence does not sweep her boy from his feet, and prove disastrous to all the elements of a noble integrity.

Is it easy to conceive of anything more dismal, or more to be regretted, than that of a boy going down into dishonesty and vice and crime through the counsel of his own mother — or if not through her direct counsel, through her implied assent? When Jehoram was dead, the inhabitants of Jerusalem made Ahaziah, his youngest son, king in his stead. They would have been glad to be loyal to him. Evidently there were qualities in him which commended him to the favor of the people, and this favor, so essential to his usefulness and happiness, he might have retained to the end. It only needed that he do right. But his mother took him in hand; and she who ought to have linked his destiny to the stars and made his name a name honored and luminous to the ages, plunged him down into the mire of exceptional degradation and wickedness.

His mother? Yes, his mother! "For his mother was his counselor to do wickedly." It would have been horrible had it been his father. It would have been horrible had it been his associates — such associates as princes sometimes cultivate and then cannot throw off when they become kings. It would have been horrible had it been anybody, for there is nothing in this universe that is quite so bad as persuading a human soul to flagrant wickedness. It was not any of these, however; it was his mother. It was she who bore him. It was she who nursed him. It was she whose ear was first greeted with the music of his half-articulated words. It was she who ought to have been as solicitous for his moral worth as an angel for the unstained whiteness of heaven. She it was who led him astray and helped him to join his name with her own in immortal infamy. His mother!

The mischief of being a bad mother is further emphasized by the consideration that a mother, in virtue of being just what she is, independent of any influence she may exert by positively evil counsels, is and must be so much to her child.

It is possible the poets exaggerate in their estimates of what mothers actually are to their offspring, and what they actually accomplish for them. Still, even in the coldest calculations, it must be admitted that Walter Savage Landor can not be far from right when he sings:

> Children are what the mothers are.
> No fondest father's fondest care
> Can fashion so the infant's heart
> As those creative beams that dart,
> With all their hopes and fears, upon
> The cradle of a sleeping son.
> His startled eyes with wonder see
> A father near him on his knee,
> Who wishes all the while to trace
> The mother in his future face;
> But 'tis to her alone uprise
> His waking arms; to her those eyes
> Open with joy and not surprise.

There are exceptions to this statement; one would

fain believe an increasing number of exceptions. Under the general influence of Christianity, and more particularly under the influence of Christianity in the home, more fathers are coming to share with the mothers in a motherly tenderness for children.

Here is another tribute to the high function of the mother which has its justification in a large number of examples in the past:

> The mother in her office holds the key
> Of the soul, and she it is who stamps the coin
> Of character, and makes the being, who would be a savage
> But for her gentle cares, a Christian man.

Not always is it so. Not always can the mother and the father working together, and aided as they may be by others who join forces with them in their beneficent aim, put the sure stamp of Christian character on even the most tenderly cherished child; but he knows little of human nature and little of the biography of the world's leading names, who does not accord an immense potency to the molding influence of a mother. It would be useless to institute comparisons between a mother's influence and the influence of other persons, or between a mother's influence and the influence of the same woman in other relations of life; but even the most self-distrusting mother and the most cynical critic would find it impossible successfully to deny a fact on which the ages have laid such stress.

No doubt the pre-natal influence of a mother on her child is often very great. It was not a mere accident or coincidence that Walter Scott's mother was a great lover of poetry and painting; or that Byron's mother was a proud woman, ill-tempered and violent; or that Nero's mother was a murderess; or that Napoleon's mother was a woman of prodigious energy; or that Patrick Henry's mother was a distinguished talker; or that Lord Bacon's mother was remarkable for her superior mental gifts; or that Wesley's mother had executive ability enough to manage a state; or that Washington's mother was devout and pure and true, and of the loftiest character. In an array of facts of which these are only specimens there must be something beside mere chance.

When to the pre-natal influence there is added the after-influence of instruction and association and example, which moves along in the same direction and continues without check or abatement through all the years of special susceptibility to educating efforts, nothing short of the endless ages can reveal how decisive and momentous has been the action of a mother's life and personality on the life and personality of her child. Benjamin West used to say it was a kiss of his mother which made him a painter. While a mere lad he sketched in rough outline the face of his little sister as she lay in the cradle before him. The mother saw promise in the work of the boy, and she bent down over him and kissed her approbation and her hope into his rosy cheek. Many a boy has gone bounding away to his apprenticeship, or to his books, or to his first struggle in business, because the mother has had both the wisdom and the love to speak an encouraging word at the right time. Her words were at once benedictions and inspirations.

The factors in society for which we have the least use are bad mothers. The evil influences which we find it hardest to counteract are the influences of bad mothers. All are familiar with the famous reply of Napoleon: "What is the greatest need in the French Nation?" But we cannot recall the answer too frequently, nor repeat it with too much emphasis: "Mothers." He meant, of course, good mothers, motherly mothers, faithful mothers, pure mothers, mothers who would take just pride in their sons and daughters, and do their best to train them in ways of industry and virtue and high worth. Is there anything any nation needs more? Is there anything which, were a nation to be largely wanting in it, would sooner work the ruin of a people? On no account can fathers be relieved of responsibility; but when the mothers in any land cease to be wise and pure and true, civil order in that land is near to its overthrow.

How much this nation owes to its mothers! What a different story there would have been to tell had the mothers of the Colonial period, when Massachusetts and Rhode Island and Connecticut and Virginia and Pennsylvania were in the formative stage, not been the large-minded and self-sacrificing and brave women they were! How unlike what it is would have been the record of the Revolutionary period, when it was as essential to the independence and self-government of the people that there should be large-souled and far-seeing and patriotic women to preside over the hearthstone and rule in the domestic circle, as that there should be daring and determined and liberty-loving and splendidly devoted men to take their places in legislative halls and in camps, had these women been wanting! Who knows what would have been the outcome; or rather who does not know how much more uncertain would have been the outcome, in the great Rebellion period, when there was a service of enthusiasm for the preservation of the Union to be rendered by the beloved ones who were left behind to watch and wait and toil and pray, as there was a service for manning forts and sailing ships and lying in trenches and storming breast-works and wading rivers and swamps and scaling heights and resisting assaults and sweeping enemies from the field where sabers flashed and cannon roared and shot fell like hail, to be rendered by those who went to the front, had not so many of the women of the North been made of the stuff found in the highest pattern of women in all the ages? No author can fitly tell the story of American history without devoting ample space to the high spirit and eminent virtue of our American mothers.

France needed, and still needs, mothers. Yes; but so does Germany, and so does England, and so does our own fair land; and life here and there and everywhere will move up as the mothers advance.

How sharp is the contrast between this mother and

that other mother whose name has illuminated Scripture story! Only with tender reverence can we mention Hannah. Only with shrinking horror can we take Athaliah on our lips. How fortunate Samuel! How inexpressibly unfortunate was Ahaziah! Hannah thanked God for the gift of her boy, and consecrated him early to the Lord, and helped him in his religious life and in the making of a name which has filled the centuries with fragrance. Athaliah waited upon her boy with malign influence, and turned him away from God, and aided him in securing an inheritance of undying infamy. Hannah and Athaliah — the two mothers; Samuel and Ahaziah — the two sons. The one high up in the admiration of mankind! The other down in the depths of human contempt! The one an inspiration! The other a warning! The one a good mother, and blessed with a good son, whom she sought to make better! The other a bad mother, who took her son, and, whatever his natural disposition or tendency, worked upon him and molded him till there was nothing for God to do but destroy him for his wickedness!

THE BIBLE IN THE HOME.

And these words, which I command thee this day, shall be upon thine heart; and thou shalt teach them diligently unto thy children, and shalt talk of them when thou sittest in thine house, and when thou walkest by the way, and when thou liest down, and when thou risest up. Deut. 6: 6-7.

IT is my purpose this morning to say a few words about *The Bible in the Home*. This is the thought which grows naturally out of the passage before us. According to the requirements laid upon the children of Israel,"these words" were not only to be cherished in their individual hearts, but they were to have central and honored place in the home-circle. They were to be welcomed to the hearthstone, and installed in power over the family. They were to enter into the economy of the daily domestic life of the people and to be the basis of a common and universal instruction.

As another has said: "Moses provided for a system of national education through the family; every child was to be taught to read and write; to be made acquainted with the history of his own country and of surrounding nations, and with the great national and religious law-book of the country. Parents were to be so imbued with the Word of God that this should give tone to their daily conversation and impress itself upon the very house. Only by such home-training," our author adds, "can a nation be kept true to God."

In our land and day, we have what is generally known as the common-school system — a system which we cannot cherish too fondly, nor guard too sacredly, since it contemplates the securing of a certain amount of knowledge and mental discipline to every child within the realm. Far be the day when any spirit of sectarianism shall be permitted to enter in and mar the unity and usefulness of the common-school system of the republic.

Moses had precisely the same object in mind, only he made the home the center of instruction, with parents for teachers, and the "words" God had spoken for the chief text-book. These "words" were the lessons to be diligently and faithfully impressed upon the children, the themes of familiar social intercourse, the thoughts to linger longest at night, to be greeted first in the morning; and when men went out they were not to forget them, but were still to talk about them by the way.

Now, without desiring, as may be inferred from what has already been said, to disparage in the least our modern system of education, nor wishing to modify it essentially, save in the direction of more emphasis on the moral element, I venture to insist that the missing link in the training of the present time is the Bible in the home. Just where Moses laid stress in his plan of national education is just where we need to lay stress. It is on the family and on the Word of God in the family. It is on the Bible in the home. Cast out of the school, it is all the more imperative that the facts and truths and precepts and laws of the sacred volume be taught at the fireside.

We have the Bible in the pulpit, in the Sunday-school, in the seminary. It enters as an informing element into the civil and social structure of society. To a large extent laws are based upon its moral standards. It is often quoted with reverence in halls of legislation. But the place where the Bible is pre-eminently potent and preëminently indispensable is in the home. Wherever else the Bible is or is not, it must be in the home, or the best influence on life is lost.

But let us understand just what is meant by this. For it is not enough that the Bible hold its place in the home as a mere empty parade. An elegant copy, gilt-edged, turkey-bound, double-clasped, stored away as ornamental furniture in a cold and unfrequented parlor, too ponderous for use and too rarely seen ever to disturb the conscience, does not meet the case. It must have some vital relation to the daily economy of every heart. It must be in fresh and constant use; the Book of habitual reference, study and delight. This is what is meant by the Bible in the home,—the Bible open, the Bible read, the Bible every day, the Bible year in and year out, the Bible in health as well as in sickness, in prosperity as well as in adversity, the Bible for the parents, the Bible for the children, the Bible for all together — a hope-anchor of the soul, a bow of promise against every adverse sky, an inexhaustible source of strength, a fresh and fragrant wisdom and an unfailing guide and inspiration of the soul.

The further development of this subject will lead us to notice

I. *The peculiar facilities which the home affords for the proper study of the Bible and especially for training and indoctrinating children in Scripture truths.*

Here, at the outset, it will be in place to utter protest against the notion, quite too prevalent, that the Bible, plain and simple, can not be made interesting to the little folks. It is above their comprehension, it is said, and so it is absurd to try to familiarize their minds with its stories and teachings. Of portions of the Bible and of some of the truths of the Bible, particularly in their abstract and remote relations, this doubtless is the fact. The doctrine of self-existence baffles all human comprehension. The incarnation involves principles before which a Butler or a Newton or a Bacon must stand in mute and conquered wonder. On the other hand, it is true of a great number of the doctrines of the Bible especially as they are stated in the Bible, that there is a marvelous adaptation in them to the tastes and requirements of the young. The stories and incidents, the striking illustrations, the wonderful facts, the graphic histories of individuals and nations, the simple language employed, the warnings uttered and the hopes set forth, all combine to make the Bible an attractive book to children.

It would be a very strange thing were it not so. For the sweetest invitations, the strongest appeals — if not all, yet many of them — in all the sacred book are addressed to children and youth. "Suffer little children to come unto me." Jesus had the story of His life so written that children should be drawn to Him. His singular birth, His strange career, His miracles and parables, His deep sympathy with the poor and neglected and distressed, the way He was treated, His words about the birds of the air, the flowers of the field, the vines on the hillside, the growing corn — all so simple and beautiful and touching — are eminently fitted to fascinate alert and growing minds. The facts bear out this expectation.

One day in a Sabbath-school with which I was connected, I found a little boy who was reading the Bible through by course. He was drawn to this task by the interest which the simple, unexplained narrative had awakened in his mind. With many of the leading facts and incidents he was perfectly familiar, so attractive and impressive had they proved to him. It is not to be supposed that this mere lad was able to discuss and explain and reconcile the ideas of divine decrees and free agency; but he did make it clear that the way of life through Jesus Christ was level to his comprehension, and that the story of that way of life is so put in the Bible that he loved to read it.

In some respects this may be an exceptional instance. At the same time, in the case of a large majority of children, I am confident they only need to be led and kindly accompanied to manifest an interest and feel delight in reading this wonderful book.

But supposing the opposite were true, what then? Is wholesome instruction to be withheld because, forsooth, it may be distasteful? Are no truths to be communicated to a child which the child cannot at once comprehend? Must great and essential lessons be simmered down till there is no substance in them, or overborne with twaddling explanations which make them something other than what they really are?

God teaches another and better wisdom. For us all, this is a life of faith and not of seeing. In every sphere of activity, and at every period of existence, much must be believed which cannot be understood. It is not one law for the child and another for the adult, but trust largely for both alike.

It would seem sufficient warrant, therefore, for one's actions, that he do for his little ones just what God does for all — give a great many things which must be taken on trust without being fully understood. Truth is to be made as simple and interesting as possible; but care is to be taken that it remain truth,

and not be transformed into sickening nonsense.   Let
the meat be cut fine, but let it remain meat still. The
instruction given ought to be warmed, quickened,
illustrated, beautified, just as far as may be; but too
often the attempt to make truth pleasant exhausts
itself in the communication of pleasure merely.   No
good is done.

It all comes round to this: There is wanted a
larger faith in the receptive capacity of children, and
a wiser reference to their future good.   We ought
to act more on the basis of the fact that children can
and do think.   The young mind is a virgin soil.   If
good seed be dropped into it, and planted deep, under God's sunshine and moisture, there will be sure
to be fruit in the future.

In the training of children there must be a policy
of forward-looking.   Ultimate advantage is to domi-
nate immediate pleasure.

Not long ago, I heard an intelligent and faithful
minister say: "When I was a child my mother
taught me the catechism — taught it to me so that I
knew it by heart.   I did not like it at the time.   I
could not understand it.   For years afterwards I
thought the method a wrong one. But now, at forty,
I know it was right.   For those truths so early acquired are within me, ineradicable and imperishable,
— a fresh and bubbling spring of living water — a
fountain of light — an arm of strength and a joy forever.   I thank God," he added, "that He gave me a
mother faithful enough and far-seeing enough to lay

thus broad and deep the foundations of my religious culture." Is it not clear that this strong man would have been robbed of a prime element of strength, and defrauded of a possession more precious than gold, had not this wise and devoted mother planted seeds thus early which should in after years ripen into a substantial harvest of rich and strong and manly character?

Right here, then, is the point. It is because the home is what it is that it may be spoken of as furnishing peculiar facilities for this Bible-training. For, take the home in the true idea of it — the home in any faint degree approximate to what it ought to be — and is it not sacred?

The home is one of the earliest and divinest institutions of earth. The spot of earth it stands upon is precious. Its unity, its individuality, its whole distinctive economy are hallowed. The love and self-sacrificing devotion of parents, the reverent and obedient affection of children — these are hints of something above the earth. The heart of a child turns instinctively to the home, and knows no other place so attractive. There is the father, provident and wise, and known familiarly and loved tenderly as he is nowhere else on earth. There is the mother, patient, industrious, careful, and she loves, and still loves, with a swelling tide right on unto the end. There are the brothers and sisters, grouped in one fond circle of courteous and mutual helpers. There is the old hearthstone, around which all gather, and where the long evenings are spent in reading and social delight. There is the table, unlike all other tables, from which God's bounty is daily partaken. There is the home-room, where all constraint is removed, and where the joy and freedom of familiar intercourse reign undisputed. There is, or there ought to be, the family altar, whence ascends the incense of devout gratitude to the Heavenly Father for His infinite goodness day by day. There is the twilight window. There is the sick-room. There are the chamber of birth and the chamber of death. There are the tokens scattered up and down, and radiant with the memories of those who have gone before. There are the birthday festivals. There are the unions and reunions of severed ones — types suggestive of those higher and holier meetings Christian households shall experience beyond the valley of the shadow. There life-plans are talked over and formed. There griefs are softly whispered and hopes announced. There confidential disclosures are made. There sympathies deep and precious and true are shared. To the home the body in its feebleness and the heart in its weariness and the brain under pressure of throbbing excitement turn for refuge. God pity those who have no home! For the sun, in all his journeyings around the globe, looks down upon nothing which has gathered into itself so much unsullied purity, so much unalloyed sweetness, so much that is comforting and inspiring, as the love-sanctified home. It lies right along on the borders of the better land. No appeal comes nearer the heart than the thought of the heavenly home. The emotions which the home awakens lift the heart easily and naturally into the contemplation of divine promises and divine verities.

All this, therefore, makes of the home a golden opportunity for impressing the Word of God upon the minds of children. The home atmosphere, so transfigured and fraught with love, may become an easy medium for the transmission of Scripture facts and truths. These home sentiments and affections can be used as wings on which to bear the soul to loftier and serener heights. The joys and delights of the home may be woven into a garment of beauty with which to dress up the doctrines of divine grace. The sweet love-light of the home may be thrown upon the Bible to lend to it the attractiveness of sacred association. The baptism of twilight moments and Sabbath hours may be made to rest upon the words of revelation in such a way that they shall stand out and apart in the mind ever after.

This opportunity of the home has only to be used in order to sanctify it to sure and precious results. Both parents ought to use it, the father as well as the mother. I know of no teaching in the Word of God, nor in what seems to be the common sense and the common equities of the case, which exempts the father from his fair share of loving endeavor in this direction.

At the same time it is the mother who is the natural priestess of the home. She it is, who with her child upon her knee can preach with an effectiveness which no pulpit can command. To her child she has surely been called of God to preach. Her ordination has not been by the laying on of the hands of presbytery, but by decree of the Most High. She with her fine instinct of love, she as the natural center of home confidences, she with her inexhaustible ingenuity of love, she in the mellow hush of the holy hour when lisping prayers are guided and confessional is opened for burdened little souls, she when griefs cry to her for soothing, and fancied wrongs demand maternal arbitration and redress, and weary little feet turn toward her for rest, and aching little heads bend over on her bosom for repose, she with all that is sacred and pure and ennobling in the thought of home and with mother-love to enforce her teaching — she can take this Word of life in her hand, and make its stories and heavenly lessons so beautiful and winning that the eyes shall never weary of gazing on them, nor the heart grow impatient of the burden of their memory. How many mothers are there working in this way with their children?

Sabbath-schools, private schools, public schools, churches, no matter how good they may be, can not take the place of wise and patient and loving instruction in the Word of God in the home.

II. *The Bible used habitually and reverently in the home, in the way just now indicated, used as text-book from which to impart and receive instruction in the things pertaining to God and a right life, tends to exert an influence on the home which is above estimate.*

This proposition, it will be perceived, differs from the foregoing one, in that it turns the thought of the Bible in the home squarely around; and under it, instead of thinking of the facilities which the home affords for the proper study of the Bible and especially for training and instructing children in the truths of the Holy Scriptures, we shall be led to consider how this kind of instruction reacts upon the home, and aids in making each home where this policy of Bible-teaching is pursued an ideal home.

Not all homes are ideal. On the contrary, there are few ideal homes. There are few homes where all the arrangements and all the relations and all the intercourse and all the influences exerted and felt, fill out the lines of the picture just drawn of a home in which there is nothing but sweetness and light. Taking the world as it is, there are many hearthstones around which no heavenly influences hover. Instead of being pervaded with an atmosphere in which the thoughts of the young are easily lifted God-ward, what multitudes of homes there are which must needs be changed in all their inner economy before they can be made to suggest anything really divine! The parents are not disciples of the Lord Jesus Christ. There is no family altar. The children never hear the father's voice invoking the divine blessing at table. When the little ones go

to rest there is no hushed moment in which the
mother bends over them, and with sweet guidance
fore-utters for their lisping tongues the precious peti-
tion which John Quincy Adams used to say he never
failed to repeat on retiring:

> Now I lay me down to sleep,
> I pray thee, Lord, my soul to keep.

No in-dweller and no passer-by is ever saluted
with the melody of the old time-sanctified Psalms
and hymns, which have so much power to cheer the
heart and chasten the spirit.   Standing in the midst
of them, one is not made to feel that the light of
heaven has ever broken through, and touched them
with supernal illuminations and glories.   They may
be homes of wealth or poverty, but they are alike in
suggesting the absence of a loving recognition of
God.   There is the lack in them of the beauty of
holiness, and one misses the perfume of the unseen
world, whose fragrant atmosphere it is possible to
breathe here and now.

It would not be right to say that there is no love
in these homes, for in many of them there is love,
tender and true.   It would not be right to say there
is no elevated sentiment, and no interest in good
morals, and no joy in many of these homes; for this,
again, would not be true.   But there is no sweet
sense of God, and no effort to organize the home-
life around the central thought of Christ and His will.

Now, it will require but little reflection to see that
the Bible, if it can only be fairly installed in the home,
is adapted in all its teachings and tendencies to ac-

complish the transformation and sanctification of the home, and take it far on towards the ideal.

1. *First, then, the Bible in the home, in the sense already defined, dignifies and ennobles the home by certifying to its divine origination.*

Men fall easily into the notion, in effect at least, that the family relation is merely a convenience of civilization; and that it finds its warrant in the habits and customs of the world. But the Bible shows that the family relation, beginning with the relation of husband and wife, is a divine institution. It is God who setteth the solitary in families. The family dates back to the Garden. It was established at the creation of man and woman, and when the soul was in its innocency. In the fall of man the sacredness of the marriage relation suffered; but like the human heart the household is to be redeemed and elevated until God's image is clearly on it.

When men can be made to realize this, it places the home on a broader and firmer basis than that of a simple business contract entered into for temporary convenience or advantage or pleasure. For to realize this is to see that the home has not grown up out of the passions and appetites of the earth, but that it has come down from God out of heaven, and has on it the stamp of the wisdom and love of the Infinite Father.

What a difference it would make in countless homes just to start with this idea of God at the outset and at the basis and at the heart of the family relation! With this fact dominant, would there be so much infidelity of husband to wife and of wife to husband — so many marital farces — so many awful marital tragedies enacted? Few men ever get this idea thoroughly into them without the Word of God to impart it. With the Bible in the home, faithfully and reverently studied, it would hardly be possible for anybody not to have this idea.

2. *The Bible in the home tends to lift the every-day life of the home to a higher plane, and to make it, in all its ongoings and appointments, more harmonious and blessed.*

The Bible, for instance, lends new sacredness to parents and new dearness to children. It binds heart to heart with closer tie. It increases the obligations and quickens the sympathies of every member of the household. It opens new sources of domestic joy and enhances every material good. It makes gray hairs more venerable and innocent childish prattle more sweet. It informs the simple songs which are sung with a diviner melody. It freights the conversation with grander themes. It elevates every thought to a higher level. It furnishes the strongest of all motives to harmony, forbearance, patience and mutual love. The precepts which it lays down for the guidance of husbands and wives, of fathers and mothers, of sons and daughters, would bring into the world much of the love and harmony and bliss of heaven. In the simple injunctions of kindness one to another and of entreaties and warnings in re-

gard to little things which the Bible lays down,
there are influences conservative of mutual forbearance and love and joy above price.

This is of great consequence. For, after all, more
frequently than otherwise, is it not the little foxes
which spoil the grapes of domestic felicity? The
story of many a wreck of married love is told by
Moore when he sings:

> Something light as air — a look,
>   A word unkind or wrongly taken —
> Oh! love, that tempests never shook,
>   A breath, a touch like this hath shaken.
> And ruder words will soon rush in
> To spread the breach that words begin;
> And eyes forget the gentle ray
> They wore in courtship's smiling day;
> And voices lose the tone that shed
> A tenderness round all they said;
> Till fast declining one by one,
> The sweetnesses of love are gone,
> And hearts, so lately mingled, seem
> Like broken clouds, or like the stream
> That smiling left the mountain's brow,
>   As though its waters ne'er could sever,
> Yet, ere it reach the plain below,
>   Breaks into floods that part forever.

As no other book, the Bible is suited to lay a restraining force on these incipient outbreaks.

Then, in connection with this thought of the Bible
in the home, consider the sweet and solid comfort
there is in it,— in its invitations, in its promises, in its
encouragements, in its lofty standards of conduct for
aspiring or perplexed or weary or suffering ones,
whether parents or children. To one who has long

been wont to consult and ponder its teachings, how indispensable does the old Book seem! How do households get on in which it is never opened; in which the twenty-third Psalm is never read nor sung; in which the Sermon on the Mount is as though it were written in an unknown tongue; in which St. Paul's immortal chapter on love and his immortal chapter on the resurrection and the incomparable section in his Epistle to the Romans in which he demonstrates the glorious deliverance all believers in Christ have from the law, are never permitted to quicken the soul; in which the apocalyptic vision of unutterable glory, which John saw at Patmos, never unfolds its splendors; in which the unrivaled majesty of the Book of Job and the fathomless wisdom of the Book of Proverbs lie sealed and neglected from year to year; in which the discourses in the upper chamber — so unlike all other discourses ever delivered — and that wonderful intercessory prayer that must stand out by itself alone through all the ages, are counted as naught; in which there is no familiarity with the names and characters of apostles and prophets and martyrs, the holy men and the sainted women of old; how, let it be asked again, do these households get on; and how do they bear their burdens, and how do they meet their disappointments, and how do they find the comfort they need when dark shadows fall and circles break and dear, sweet voices are hushed?

It is a beautiful tribute which Mrs. Hemans pays to the influence of the Bible in the home:

What household thoughts around thee, as their shrine,
Cling reverently!   Of anxious looks beguiled,
My mother's eyes upon thy page divine
Were daily bent; her accents, gravely mild,
Breathed out thy love; whilst I, a dreamy child,
On breeze-like fancies wandered oft away,
To some lone tuft of gleaming spring-flowers wild,
Some fresh-discovered nook for woodland play,
Some secret nest; yet would the solemn word,
At times, with kindlings of young wonder heard,
Fall on my wakened spirit, there to be
A seed not lost; for which in darker years,
O Book of Heaven! I pour with grateful tears
Heart-blessings on thy holy dead, and thee.

3. *In the third place, the Bible in the home, faithfully and reverently studied, is the best safeguard of the moral purity of the home.*

In making this statement am I not striking far over into a territory which needs to be cultivated? Is not this thought of what will best keep our homes clean and sweet a suitable climax to all that has gone before?   For, quite independent of all other objects to be gained, is it not time that something substantial be done to deepen the public sense of the inviolability and sacredness of our domestic life?   With secret inroads opened from every quarter against the welfare of the home; with the demand for divorces multiplying; with parents losing control over their children, and licentiousness creeping into our domestic and social life to poison and destroy, in so many guises; with men who are known to have been untrue to their own obligations, and to have broken up the homes of their neighbors, petted and honored in clubs and in business and political circles, and heartily welcomed into fastidious society, as though the most flagrant violation of the seventh commandment were a mere passing misdemeanor, to be waived into forgetfulness, — is there not a call very imperative for a higher conception and a diviner influence and a holier restraint to enter into the economy of all our homes? When the bonds of husband and wife can be snapped asunder like strands of tow, and hearthstones are no longer sacred to the pledges of a pure and faithful life, and the practices of Mormons are followed without any such pretense of justification as the Mormons feel obliged to offer to the world, surely something effective must be done to reverse these corrupt tendencies.

What better than the laws — what, indeed, half so good as the laws and the ordinances and the precepts and the uncompromising principles of the Word of God? Men and women and children do sometimes break through all restraint, and run off into wild prodigal ways; but it will not be an easy thing nor will it be a common thing to become recreant to virtue and sink down into rioting and crime, if the home in which one is brought up, or has his daily life, is saturated with the spirit of the Holy Scriptures, and it is a customary thing to ponder on the truths and duties taught us in revelation.

All these statements and suggestions come to focus in this practical counsel: Give the Bible the place it ought to occupy in your homes. Enthrone it in power. Let not the daily newspaper nor the popular magazine nor the most eminent standard author come between you and the daily reading of God's Word.

Some of you, I doubt not, have precious memories of homes where the Bible was a reverenced and studied book. You can hear the tones of the father's voice as he read in the morning, and recall the awfulness with which the old prophetic periods were clothed, or the delight with which the precious promise fell upon your ear. You can see a beloved mother garnering strength and courage and consolation day by day from the psalms and beatitudes. You know the words which were taught you then have clung to your memory, and will be part and parcel of you through all eternity. Now, by all that is sacred in these recollections, by all the love you bear your little ones, by all the terrors of the judgment before which we must all appear and meet the record of our lives, I beseech you to be faithful in your own homes, faithful to God and to those whom God has committed to your care.

It will soon be too late. When these children have grown up and gone out into their life-work, let it not be theirs to say: "I might have been made familiar with the Bible and its blessed teachings; and through the influence of truths thus learned might perhaps have been led into an assured hope of eternal life in Christ; but my parents were not faith-

ful, and the Book divine had no honored place in
the economy of my early home." Nor give them
occasion to go on and say further: "Pains were
taken that I might know how to dance well, to dress
well, to buy and sell, to travel, and that I might be
duly impressed with the need of self-reliance and
energy and foresight; but the Word of God was left
out of the influences to which I was daily subjected.
Sabbaths with their sacred privileges came and went;
evening succeeded evening; childhood slipped away,
then youth passed into early maturity, and the freedom of dependent years gave place to the cares and
burdens of responsible life; yet the Bible was not
opened before me, and I was not taught at home to
revere its teachings and be guided by its precepts."
Do not give your children occasion to rise up hereafter and say that.

You may not be able to leave your children wealth
or the inheritance of a great name or eminent
social advantages; but you can leave them the results
of fidelity and precious memories of devotion to the
holy task of trying to make them know what God
says to us in the Old and New Testaments, and what
He wants us to believe and to do and to be.

CHRISTIANITY IN THE LIGHT OF THE PARLIAMENT OF RELIGIONS.

And in none other is there salvation, for neither is there any other name under heaven, that is given among men, whereby we must be saved. Acts. 4: 12.

QUITE likely it will always be a question in the minds of some whether it was wise or not to attempt to hold a parliament of religions. But whatever conclusions may be reached concerning the scheme in its original inception, and whatever its influence may prove to be on subsequent thought and life, the parliament has actually been convened, and its proceedings have gone into history, to be examined and estimated like any other occurrences and events of the past.

But now that it is over and there has been time for study and sober reflection, it is only natural that those of us who have turned our eyes away to the incarnate Son of God and have fixed our hopes for salvation on the crucified Christ, should, — not in alarm, nor even with any special degree of solicitude, but with a justifiable interest in the outcome of any comparisons which may have been instituted between the religion of Jesus and any other religions to which men adhere, — ask after the bearing of this unique gathering on **our** own faith.

In the light, then, of this parliament of religions, how fares it with our Christianity, and how does our Christianity look to us after having been subjected to this series of tests? Does the *suffering Saviour* still seem to be the Lamb slain from the foundation of the world, and the one ground of reconciliation to God?

The answers to this question are manifold.

In general it may be said that Christianity emerges from this wide review of the religions of the world as Daniel came out of the den of lions, not only "with no manner of hurt" upon it, but freshly indorsed and accredited to mankind as the one religion through which our race is to be saved and the kingdom of God is to be set up on the earth. Never did Christianity appear to me to be so large, — so large on the God-ward side and so large on the man-ward side — to hold in it so much truth and love and saving power, and to be so manifestly a divine system, as when it was placed there side by side with Buddhism and Brahminism and Confucianism and Mohammedanism and Parseeism, and the story of its claims and achievements was set forth by such men as Bishop Dudley and Professor Wilkinson and Joseph Cook and Post and Washburn and Mills and Pentecost.

More especially it may be said that Christianity was shown by this comparison to be the only religion which faces all the facts and takes in all the conditions of the problem which religion is required to solve.

There are three questions which must be answered,

and answered intelligently and satisfactorily, by any system of faith which aspires to secure and hold the confidence of men who have come into a full realization of their own needs.

The first concerns God — His existence, His personality, His character and His relation to the universe and to law and to life.

The second concerns man — his nature, his place in the world, his moral condition, his privileges, his duty and his destiny.

The third concerns the way in which men who have sinned, and by sinning have fallen out of harmony with God, may be restored to harmony with God and the joy of His fellowship.

Now it may be conceded that these Oriental religions hold in them the idea of God. Not all of them hold this idea in the same form, nor with the same distinctness of conception; but they hold it. For the idea of God is a universal idea. Whether men come into their knowledge of God through what has been called the faculty of God-consciousness or by a process of induction or by the witnessing of the Divine Spirit, it does not especially concern us just now to consider; but this knowledge is abroad among the nations of the earth. Indeed, this is the express avowal of the Scriptures. Paul bore testimony to this fact there at Lystra when he said that though the nations in the generations gone by had been suffered to walk in their own ways, yet God had not left Himself without witness in that He had done good, and given rain from heaven and fruitful seasons, and filled the hearts of men with food and gladness. He bore the same testimony in those remarkable words of his in the epistle to the Romans: "For the wrath of God is revealed from heaven against all ungodliness and unrighteousness of men, who hold down the truth in unrighteousness; because that which may be known of God is manifest in them; for God manifested it unto them. For the invisible things of Him since the creation of the world are clearly seen, being perceived through the things that are made, even His everlasting power and divinity; that they may be without excuse." On the basis of our own sacred writings, these adherents of the ethnic faith may come to us and say: "Inasmuch as we are creatures made in the image of God, and are living our lives here in this world of God, you must concede to us the instincts of religion and the capacity for religion and the possibility of our possessing some knowledge, even though it be very imperfect and vague, of God both as Creator and Father." But it is needless to say here in this presence, though doubtless there are places where it will have to be said over and over again, that the conception of God, especially in the higher and more tender relations in which He has revealed Himself to us in His Word and in the life and character of His Son, which was entertained by these representatives of the dominant religions of China and Japan and India and Arabia falls far below the requirements and aspirations of the soul. The well defined personality, the exalted holiness, the condescending love, the sweet brooding care with which the disciples of Jesus have become accustomed to associate the name of God are wanting; or if not altogether, yet largely wanting.

In the Oriental religions, as opened out in the parliament, there was also a clear acknowledgment of some sort of very sad derangement in the condition of mankind. But there was a disposition, so marked as to be noticeable all through the proceedings, to fight shy of calling this derangement by the ugly name of "sin." One of these brilliantly attired representatives who spoke in behalf of "mild Hinduism" ventured on one occasion to use the word "sin;" but he did it to say: "It is a sin to call a man a sinner." This was one of the grounds of affiliation between these Orientals and our Liberal Christians. Neither of them has much stomach for a word which implies guilt and condemnation and holds every human soul in the awful grip of a violated law. "Unintentional stumbling," "imperfection in development," "incidents connected with growth," "short-sightedness," "natural mistakes" are the phrases which suit them a great deal better than this old harsh word "sin."

This is one of the tendencies of the time — to tone down the stress on sin and to call it something else than sin. These Orientals fell in with the popular currents, — with the currents which are set in motion by our ethical-culture societies and our easy-method reformers and our milk-and-water liberalism, and like our own quacks they tried to show that the disease with which humanity is affected is not so organic and fatal as some would make us think by calling it by another and a softer name. But this malady is sin. This disability is sin. This sad derangement of human life as witnessed all over the world, and witnessed to a degree which is unutterably mournful in lands where the Gospel has not done its work, is a derangement which is due to sin. No man has uttered the last word which is to be said concerning the moral and spiritual condition of the race till he has uttered this word sin.

These men of the Oriental faiths come to us and tell us they know God, — know Him just as well as Christians know Him. Very well then. That fixes guilt. That justifies the charge that all men are under condemnation and are verily guilty before God. This is exactly Paul's ground. Men everywhere are "without excuse" — are justly held under condemnation — because men everywhere have some knowledge of God. Just in the ratio, therefore, in which these disciples of other systems made it clear that they have some correct knowledge of God they made it clear that they are sinners and are justly held responsible for the transgression of the law.

But here comes in the further inquiry, and it is an inquiry on which it is simply impossible to place too much emphasis: How is a man who has some knowledge of God and wishes to have more, but who is conscious, whatever others may tell him, that he is a sinner because he has broken the laws of God, — to find his way into terms of peace with God and be able to stand there face to face with God and feel that in the highest sense with which the words can be freighted God is his Father and he is God's child? Must it be by the long process of incarnations and re-incarnations? Must it be by the dead lift of a strugling will? Must it be by a series — nobody knows how near to endless — of penances and good works? How is Zaccheus to come into the new and higher fellowship which his soul suddenly craves? How is the woman at the well to put off the old, miserable, grimy life and to put on the new life of righteousness? How is the thief on the cross to find his way all at once through the gates of Paradise? How may John Newton roll off the heavy burden of his wicked past, and go on glad and radiant in the consciousness that his name is in the book of life? How may John Bunyan secure the courage and help he needs to turn square about and walk that immortal pilgrimage of his to the celestial city? How may any soul anywhere get up out of its sins into the favor and fellowship of God? What answer has Buddhism? What answer has Brahminism? What, Confucianism? What, Mohammedanism? What, Parseeism? Is there no answer which these religions can give? Is there no forgiveness with God? Must the poor publican stand afar off and beat his breast and cry in vain for God to be merciful to him a sinner? Is there no im-

mediate relief, no sweet peace, no uplift right here
and now into the joys and triumphs of the endless
life for Zaccheus and the woman at the well and the
thief on the cross and John Newton and John Bunyan? But what answer has Christianity? Christianity has this answer, — Christ. Christ there on Calvary, bearing the sins of the sinner in his own body
and dying that those who are afar off may be made
nigh through His blood, that those who are alienated
in their minds and hearts may be restored to allegiance, and that those who are under condemnation
may be taken out from their condemnation and given
a standing in righteousness, He is our peace. There
is therefore now no condemnation to them who are in
Christ. By the simple act of faith in the crucified
Christ the whole outlook is changed at once. The
sinner becomes God's true child.

That the comparative value of the Oriental faiths
for saving sinners and bringing them over into harmony with God, is not here put too low, may be seen
by bringing forward the testimony of a single witness whose competency to speak on such a subject
will not be called in question. This is the eminent
Monier-Williams. There are few men now living,
and in all probability few men have ever lived, better
qualified to pronounce upon the comparative merits
of the ethnic religions and of Christianity.

There is the more significance to be attached
to the judgment to which this man has finally ar-

rived, because, at the beginning, he was very strongly inclined to favor the non-Christian religions. In his "Origin and Growth of Religions" Müller made very clear what was the trend of his thinking on the subject. When Monier-Williams began to investigate Hinduism and Brahminism, he was, it would not be too much to say, sharply prejudiced in their favor. The discovery of brilliant flashes of thought and expressions of eager desire for better things amid the general darkness greatly quickened his admiration. Now he franklyconfesses his mistak e, and denounces "the flabby, jelly-fish toleration which refuses to see and acknowledge the decided superiority of Christianity to all these other religions." At the anniversary of a missionary society in London he said: "Go, in your Master's name; go forth into all the world; after studying all the false religions, fearlessly proclaim to suffering humanity the plain, the unchangeable, the eternal facts of the Gospel of Christ, — nay, I might almost say, the stubborn, the unyielding, the inexorable facts of the Gospel. Let it be absolutely clear that Christianity can not, must not, be watered down to suit the palates of Hindu, Parsi, Buddhist, Confucianist or Mohammedan. Whosoever wishes to pass from the false religion to the true, can never hope to do so by the rickety planks of compromise. He must leap the gulf in faith, and the living Christ will spread his everlasting arms beneath, and land him safe on the *eternal rock*." On addressing the British and Foreign

Bible Society, he gave unqualified endorsement to Christianity, in language as strong. After characterizing the Veda and other sacred books, he went on to affirm: "They all say salvation must be purchased, be bought with a price; the sole price, the sole purchase money, must be our own works and deservings. Our own Holy Bible, *our* Sacred Book of the East, is from beginning to end a protest against this doctrine. Good works are indeed enjoined, but they are only the outcome of a grateful heart, only a thank-offering, the fruits of faith. They are never the ransom money of the true disciples of Christ. . . Let us teach Hindus, Buddhists, Mohammedans that there is only one Sacred Book of the East that can be their mainstay in that awful hour when they shall pass into the unseen world. It is the Sacred Book which contains that faithful saying worthy to be received of all men, women and children, not merely of us Christians, but of all men, women and children everywhere, — 'Christ Jesus came into the world to save sinners.'"

On the strength of testimony like this may it not be affirmed, — must it not be affirmed — with new emphasis that it is Jesus Christ alone who saves sinners? But how willing He is to save! How prompt! How thorough, too, in His salvation!

Thus Christianity faces all the facts and takes in all the conditions of the problem which religion is required to solve. It makes God known in the attractiveness of His Fatherhood as He is not known outside the circle of Christian revelation and instruction. It discloses man to himself so that he sees and feels what his real and crying needs are. Having shown men where they are and what they are, Christianity opens to them a way of escape from sin and of return to the Father. Christianity through its crucified Christ saves sinners. It saves them at once, and it saves them unto the uttermost. If any of these other religions, oriental or ethical or liberal, which had any word to say on the platform of the parliament, has any method by which a sinner can be saved, and saved at once, and saved unto the uttermost, great pains must have been taken to keep the secret.

Christianity, to consider the matter for a little from another point of observation, as studied in the light of the parliament of religions and looked at in the whole range of its influence and power, has made it evident that it stands at the head not only, but at the head by a vast intervening space, of all the religions of which we have any knowledge in the regenerating energy with which it works at the heart of humanity.

A distinguished German writer has said that at the beginning of the Christian era there were three great and distinct ends to be gained in order to bring society into harmony with itself and put all conditions at their best. The first was to overcome race prejudices and distinctions, and lead all nations and kindreds and tribes and tongues to feel that they were of one blood. The second was to overcome class prejudices and distinctions and bring the high and the low, the rich and the poor, into a mutual recognition and fellowship. The third was to overcome sex prejudices and distinctions, and elevate woman into an equality of privilege with man, so that both might advance hand in hand. This was a large scheme, — large and beneficent.

But singularly enough, so this writer goes on to show, the Apostle Paul was able to condense this whole program of moral reform and progress into a couple of verses in two of his letters. Speaking in his Epistle to the Galatians of the way in which faith in Christ lifts all souls into a common sonship to God, he says: "There can be neither Jew nor Greek, there can be neither bond nor free, there can be no male and female; for ye are all one in Christ Jesus." Urging in his Epistle to the Colossians all followers of Jesus to walk worthy of their new creation in the image of God, he uses this similar language: "Where there can not be Greek and Jew, circumcision, and uncircumcision, barbarian, Scythian, bondman, freeman; but Christ is all and in all." Here we have it then, — race distinction and prejudice — Greek and Jew, barbarian and Scythian — swept away and lost in the love of Christ; class distinction and prejudice — neither bond nor free — swept away and lost in the love of Christ; sex distinction and prejudice — no male and female — swept away and lost in the love of Christ.

These were the objective points toward which Christianity was set at the very beginning. It was to save men through the grace of God in Christ Jesus; but through saved men it was to inaugurate a condition of real brotherhood, and unite heart to heart and home to home and community to community and nation to nation and race to race in a way to foretoken and condition the ushering in of the New Jerusalem.

These are the lines along which our Christianity has been moving since the Day of Pentecost. Under the influence of the truth and spirit of Christianity the nations of the earth have been drawing closer and closer together, and they were never so bound up in the sense and obligation of unity as they are at this hour. His fetters have fallen from the slave, and wherever Christianity is permitted to bear sway there is no bondman to curse the earth with the sweat of his unrequited toil. Woman has come to her estate of larger liberty and freely granted opportunity, and life is sweeter. Much remains to be done. As yet only faint beams of the millennial dawn are visible. There are horrible wrongs to be righted. There are injustices which cry to heaven for redress. The poor and the ignorant and the wayward and the vicious and the criminal are multitudinous. For good men there is no earthly rest in sight.

Meanwhile how is it with these oriental religions? What have their adherents been doing? What have they been doing in the sphere of art and science?

What have they been doing in the sphere of home and social life and good government? What have they been doing for woman? What, to overcome caste? What, to promote social purity and truth-speaking and honesty in the transactions of business? What, to displace superstition with intelligence and to elevate the common and oppressed people to a higher plane of life? What have they done to reform abuses and to improve schools and to introduce new ideas into the minds of their people and to kindle new and higher aspirations in all hearts? Let every excellence and every achievement claimed for these ethnic religions by their adherents or apologists be granted, and still the question recurs: What have these religions done along the lines here indicated? Especially what have they done in comparison with the triumphs of Christianity?

Once more we may summon one of our previous witnesses to bear his testimony. In speaking of Brahmanism, as he might, indeed, speak of these other ethnic faiths, Monier-Williams says: "The present characteristics of Brahminism are poverty, ignorance and superstition. Whatever profound thought lay about the roots of Hinduism, it held and still holds the 280,000,000 of India in the bondage of degradation, cruelty and immorality." If the testimony of competent witnesses is of any value this would seem to settle the question of the amount of moral power to be found in oriental religions.

Some of these religions get credit for merits which

are really not their own. For when set down by
their side, and allowed a little time for doing its
work, Christianity is always found to have communicated some of its ideas and some of its influences to
them. Movements among the adherents of Hinduism, like that which was represented by Mohur Roy
and Chunder Sen or that which is now represented
by Mozoomdar, derive a large part of their significance and force from the ethical and spiritual elements imported into them from Christianity. The
best conception found in the creed of the Somajes,
and the worthiest ends toward which they encourage
men to struggle are conceptions and ends which they
came to know through Christianity. Measured by
its moral force and influence there is no religion like
Christianity.

This view of Christianity, if it be the right view,
makes quick work of the claim that the Faith of Jesus
is only one of many faiths, and is no more entitled
to a superior rank in the reverent regard of mankind
than any other well articulated system of belief.
Christianity is not one of many faiths; it is the one
Faith. It is a fine thing to talk about and to grow
sentimental over; but there is no "brotherhood of
religions." There is a brotherhood in natural sonship; for all alike are made in the image of God.
There is a brotherhood of dependence; for in Him we
all of us live and move and have our being. There
is a brotherhood of need; for we are members one of
another, and no man liveth unto himself and no man

dieth unto himself. There is a brotherhood of condemnation; for all have sinned and come short of the glory of God. There is a brotherhood of radiant hope and possibility; for whosoever will may enter in and become an heir, joint with Jesus Christ, to the everlasting inheritance. But in the sense that all religions are alike of divine origin, and are equally suited to the needs of man, and equally valuable in the aid they render, there is no brotherhood of religions. Our Christianity in the revelation it makes of the personality and light and love of God, and in its methods of delivering from the guilt and bondage and corruption of sin, and in the guidance it yields and the aid it affords for the living of a right life, has no mate. It stands out by itself alone, immeasurably superior and glorious beyond comparison. It is Jesus Christ who is the light of the world. It is Jesus Christ who is the restorer of lost souls. It is Jesus Christ who puts our human hand in the hand of the Father. It is on the religion of Jesus Christ that the hopes of humanity rest.

THE DIVINE INTEREST PERSONAL TO EACH OF US.

Who loved me and gave himself for me. Gal. 2:20.
Now Jesus loved Martha, and her sister, and Lazarus.
John 11: 5.

THESE two passages unite in setting forth the same great and precious fact, though they do it from opposite points of view. In the first passage we see the Apostle individualizing the love which was shown by God in the gift of Christ to a lost world, and appropriating it to himself: "Who loved me." In the second passage we see Jesus, who is the Son of God, standing here and pouring out His love through individual channels upon individual hearts: "Now Jesus loved Martha, and her sister, and Lazarus." Hence a double justification of our one theme, which is *The Divine Interest Personal to Each of Us.*

This truth of the individualizing of God's interest in us in such way that His love is made personal to each human soul is a large one. The sweep of it, the significance of it and the power of it are very much more than we are wont to think.

Guizot, in the opening chapter of his History of Civilization, though he does not stay to discuss it, pauses long enough to raise the question whether society exists for the individual or the individual for society. Without any hesitation he gives in his adherence to the idea that society is merely the theater, the occasion, the motive and excitement, for the development of the individual. Man has a higher destiny than the state. There is more in man than can be met by any social amelioration. After society has done all it is possible for society to do for him, there still remain those higher faculties by which he elevates himself to God, to a future life and to the unknown blessings of the invisible world.

This is the Christian conception as against the materialistic or pessimistic conception. Man is the unit of value. Man is the end in view. It is to get man up into a higher condition, — all his faculties developed and cultivated to the most eminent degree, that institutions exist. The state is for man. The church is for man. The home is for man. Laws and customs and economics are for man. Whatever helps, whatever inspires, whatever society most cherishes, is for man. We have not reached the ultimate object of orderly government, of secure and comfortable domestic arrangements, of schools and colleges, of literature, of science, of art, of wholesome industries encouraged and protected, of trade and commerce carried on successfully, of the inventions and discoveries with which the world is enriched from time to time, till we have found it in man.

It looks sometimes as though states, institutions customs, laws were everything and man nothing. How men toil for food and raiment! But food and raiment are for men, and not men for food and raiment. Men toil for houses and lands; how often, indeed, do they wear themselves out in amassing these properties! But houses and lands are for men, and not men for houses and lands.

Emergencies arise when human lives, the most precious of them, and thousands upon thousands, have to be sacrificed to save the state. Some of the most thrilling pages in the histories of the nations, — Greece, Rome, England, Holland, America, are those in which are recorded the story of the heroic sacrifices made by brave souls to save the commonwealth from overthrow and ruin.

But the ultimate end of it all is the good of men. For states, with all that is valuable in them, with all their restraining and directing power, are for men. We talk often of sacrifices for the church, and quite likely we sometimes make the impression that the church is of more consequence than the individual; but the church again is for men.

But this is not the final truth. It is not merely men in the mass — mankind — as against the agencies and organizations by which the rights of men are guarded and their welfare is promoted, toward which the divine interest goes out; but God takes men and loves them and aids them one by one. He individualizes His interest, and He makes His regard and His watchfulness personal to each of us. Jesus said not only "*Our* Father" but "*My* Father." God looks down upon us and says not only "My *chil-*

dren" but "My *child*." How nature singles out and individualizes things! It is this rose, that violet. The Psalmist had the same notion of God and the stars: "He calleth them all by name." The prophet Isaiah expresses the same thought, and then adds: "Not one faileth." In this universe there is nothing which is not individualized to God.

This was the Apostle's view of the great and precious salvation of Jesus Christ. There are not wanting passages in the Bible — a large number of them — in which the love of God as shown in the gift of His Son to die on the cross is generalized and made to include the entire race. "God so loved *the world*." The love of God is exceeding broad.

> There's a wideness in God's mercy
> Like the wideness of the sea.

The provision He has made for our redemption covers all. But Paul was not content to be swallowed up in the mass. He did not like to think of himself as absorbed in the aggregate of redeemed souls and having no more individuality in the regard of God than the trees of the forest have in the vision of one who looks upon them from the height of some distant mountain-top. So he made the whole transaction intensely personal to himself. "For I through the law died unto the law, that I might live unto God. I have been crucified with Christ; yet I live; and yet no longer I, but Christ liveth in me; and that life which I now live in the flesh I live in faith, the faith which is in the Son of God, who loved me and gave Himself for me." It is all personal.

It is like a mother with her children. For the purpose of general statement she groups them all under the sweetly sheltering word — "mine." Still in her thought and heart they are all individualized. Her experience with each is a distinct experience. The story of each as it is treasured up in her memory is a distinct story. To speak one name in that circle is to open one volume. To speak another name is to open another volume. From first born to last born there will be some reason why the mother's heart goes out to each with a peculiar interest.

The Apostle knew Christ died for all. He did not claim for himself anything more than others who believed in Christ might claim. Each of the Galatian or Ephesian or Corinthian Christians to whom he wrote might appropriate his language, if he wished, and use it with the same fitness. Peter might say: "Who loved *me* and gave Himself for *me*." John might say: "Who loved *me* and gave Himself for *me*." There never has been a genuine disciple — there never will be one — who might not take these words in his mouth and utter them with the stress of an absolute assurance: "Who loved *me* and gave Himself for *me*." Just as a man stands and sees the light of the sun falling straight in on him, though the world all about him is flooded with the same light and warmth, and says: "It is for *me*," — so a disciple may stand in front of the cross and jubilantly exclaim: "It is for *me*."

Not too much can the fact be emphasized that the regard of God is not for an abstraction called humanity, nor for a concrete mass; it is for persons, individuals. God loves humanity; but He reaches the whole by reaching the constituent parts. He keeps the heavens studded with stars and the universe aflame with light by kindling individual stars. He rears vast forests by planting and nourishing individual trees. He makes landscapes rich with wealth of grass and flower and shrub and climbing vine by having a thought for each spire of grass and each plant and each unfolding bud and each swelling leaf. The landscape is the aggregate of all the individual objects composing it. But there is not a tiny rootlet which is not fed by itself. There is not a bursting germ of vegetation which does not have its own drop of dew or rain; nor a flower without its own beam of light.

If now we take this general statement of the way in which God individualizes His regard and makes it personal to each one of us, we shall find it helpful in many particulars. We shall find it helpful — sometimes as a restraint, but helpful always in the fact that it brings God very near to our lives.

I. *There is comfort in the thought that through this individualizing of His regard and making it personal to each, God suits His grace to the particular temperament and needs of men.*

No two persons are exactly alike. There are duplicate elements in men, and in some particulars a good portrait of one would be sure to have enough in it of family likeness to be a good portrait of all. But there are points of difference, and these points of difference are so marked that they always have to be taken into account. There are odd people. There are thin-skinned people. There are egotistic people; and there are over-modest people. There are quick people; and there are slow people. There are people who suffer long and are kind; and there are people who are all the time on the watch for something to offend them. There are people with whom one can be frank and open; and there are people before whom one has to walk as on eggs. Temperaments are multitudinous in their variety; and habit often confirms and strengthens what was a peculiarity of original endowment.

It would take a great many volumes to hold all that has been written about the unlikeness of the Bethany sisters. Of course Lazarus differed from each of them; for who ever knew a brother who didn't differ from his sisters? But the unlikeness between Mary and Martha was very sharp. Mary was of the meditative type; Martha was of the active and stirring sort. Mary thought nothing was of so much importance and so rewarding, as to sit, when there was opportunity, at the feet of Jesus and learn of Him and drink in His spirit. Martha had a constraining sense of things to be done; she was prompt and full of activity; and she wanted everybody else to be moving and doing what seemed to her a full share of the work which pressed. Mary was calm. She had the repose of soul characteristic of one who has entered into the secret of the Lord and rests in peace. Martha was nervous, impatient, distracted. She was industrious; she was careful; she was eager to lend assistance; but her life was more on the surface; and what occupied her to such an extent she thought ought to occupy others. "Lord, dost thou not care that my sister did leave me to serve alone?" She was cumbered about much serving; she was anxious and troubled about many things; and she complained because she did not have the aid she thought she ought to have. We all know the answer to her complaint. "One thing is needful; Mary hath chosen the good part, which shall not be taken away from her." There is a tone of rebuke in our Lord's reply — this must be admitted. At the same time His words are not so much words of rebuke as of explanation and tender justification of the conduct of her who sat at His feet and entered into such profound sympathy with Him in His character and purpose.

But the unlikeness of each to the other was no bar to the love of Christ. Martha had her individuality. Mary had her individuality. From all we can discover Lazarus had his individuality; yet Jesus loved them all. "He loved Martha, and her sister, and Lazarus."

As in this instance, so in all instances. The divine love suits itself to the peculiarities of men and women. Men often have constitutional traits which are exceedingly disagreeable and which make it very hard to get on with them. They may be opinionated or fussy or crabbed or effusive to a trying degree. They may have glaring faults, and reach pitches in their hobby-riding and in their personal bearing toward others, which make them intolerable to all save those who are obliged to bear with them. But God knows how, and has the patience, to adapt Himself to all that is singular in these characters. Like a brook in a mountain district, which winds in and out among the rocks and creeps on through the gnarled roots of the obtruding trees and dashes at a leap over the jutting ledges and makes its way, now in silence and now in song, over all inequalities of surface and past all obstructions, to the sea, God can press in past all that is eccentric in a man and get by all the sharp turns in his make-up. The world may be impatient with us for our peculiarities; but — God knoweth our frame.

II. *It is good to know that God is near to us, and feels a personal interest in us, in the work, whatever it may be, which it falls to our lot to do.*

In the average life there is a deal of work which is out-and-out drudgery. It is hard and wearisome and often repulsive. In the school, in the home, in the store and office and mill, on the farm, in the mine, at sea, there are services to be performed which nobody would undertake were there not necessity. It taxes nerves and offends taste and crucifies the flesh to do these things.

How much of this work falls to the lot of mothers to whose wisdom and patience is committed the training of children! How much to clerks and apprentices who mean to know their business from top to bottom and in all its ins and outs!

Then outside of this, when men and women put their hands to benevolent tasks and reform movements, and try to make individual lives better and homes better and cities better and nations better and races better, how much there is to annoy and weary and discourage! It is often a marvel to me how leaders and lawgivers like Moses and prophets like Jeremiah, how the Ezras and Nehemiahs, how the Daniels and Pauls, how the Luthers and Wesleys, how the Frys and Howards, how the Wilberforces and Garrisons manage to hold fast to their aims from the moment when their eyes are first opened to what is to be done and their hearts are kindled into enthusiasm, to the final hour when they fold their hands and fall asleep.

In all these spheres, in one's own personal work and in the larger services which are undertaken for the elevation of humanity, there is always much to quench zeal, to overburden mind and body and to make one feel at times, at least, whether the energy and courage one may possess are a match for the work required.

But when we think of ourselves as individuals toward whom the currents of the individual love of God are always flowing like incoming tides up the mouths of brooks, — of ourselves as never getting beyond the sweep of His individual care, never doing a thing in such obscurity that He does not see us and take accurate note of the spirit in which we toil and the secret aims we cherish, never bearing a burden that He does not know its exact weight and how hard it presses, never misjudged, never wrongly esti-mated, never put at disadvantage by the greed and ambition and thoughtlessness of men, without Him by our side to re-judge and re-estimate and rectify all, if not altogether for time, yet for the record of eternity, — it makes all the difference in the world. Drudgery is never again so trying. Hardness is never again so hard. Obscurity is never again so difficult to en-dure. "He loves me. He is interested in my inter-ests. If my interest moves along in the line of duty and helpful service, I can be patient and bear my burdens." So the soul reasons so soon as it becomes conscious of this individualizing of the divine re-gard.

This is the open secret of the uncomplaining fidel-ity with which a great many saintly souls keep about their tasks. They do not feel themselves to be mere indistinguishable parts of a stupendous whole on which God looks only in a kind of all-inclusive and general way. The astronomer lifts his telescope and surveys the distant star, but he is able to distinguish little save in dim and uncertain outline. God turns His eye to the earth, and He discerns separate souls, — individuals, persons, and He follows them with an individual, personal love and a sympathy tenderly suited to their individual needs. The maid scrubbing the floor of the kitchen; the street-sweeper; the sailor amid storms on the high seas; the soldier on the frontier guarding the interest of an advancing civilization; the miner down in the depths of the earth with his candle and pick; the farmer toiling under the heat of the noon-day sun; the mechanic at his bench; the engineer with eye thrust sharply forward and hand on lever, guiding his long train with its precious freight through the darkness; the teacher trying to impart knowledge and quicken aspiration in dull minds, it may be; the reformer who is sounding a note for which the age is not yet ripe; the missionary confronting the ignorance and superstition and vice of the great pagan world, — each and all of them may be sure that if there is any desire for His presence God is at hand, taking the measure of the work and noting all that is irksome and disagreeable about it and bestowing grace and strength sufficient for what is to be done. Some things could not be done at all without this consciousness; but there is no work which would not be easier could we only think of God as near to us while doing it.

It is the mother and her children over again. They are grown up and are no longer about her. They make no more a group which she can take in with a single sweep of the eye. One is in the sunny South; one is yonder amongst the mines of Colorado; one is back on the hills of New England; one is far

away across the waters in India. Their occupations
differ; and some are engaged in dignified and some
in lowly services. Some are winning wealth and
golden opinions, and some are still, as they were at
the outset, very near the bottom. But wherever they
are and whatever they are doing, the mother-heart
goes straight out to each one of them. What the
mother does imperfectly, God does perfectly. He
takes in all; but He takes in each — each separate
soul; and He has a sympathetic interest in each.

III. *This fact of a divine interest, personal to
each of us, when realized, has a marked value in
restraining from sin.*

Nothing is more common than for men to try to
persuade themselves, when they are tempted to do
wrong, that they are lost in the mass. Or, if there is
anything more common, it is the idea that when one
is associated with others in delinquencies or vices
or crimes, there is not much likelihood that the condemnation will be personal. Men sin with their
nation or their party or their guild or their church,
or they sin under the shelter of the current customs
and habits of their times; and they fancy that somehow God does not hold each individual of the number to such sharp responsibility as He would if there
were only one in place of many. Each imagines
himself to be screened in some measure behind the
others. That there is a whole company of wrong-
doers distributes or palliates the guilt, so it is conceived, and men sin with all the more confidence.

Lynching parties and wild mobs proceed on this assumption.

There may be prudential reasons, — reasons, that is, drawn from considerations of business standing and of domestic standing and regard for the opinion of social circles, as well as thought of self-respect and pride, why one who wishes to drink or throw dice, might desire to enter a saloon or a gambling resort alone, or without the knowledge of his intimate friends.

But ordinarily there will be less compunction and less sense of guilt when two or more go together. It is not an uncommon thing, even in such places as the cars, to hear young men talking freely to each other about their immoralities; and they make light of such doings on the ground that there are so many others who are addicted to the same practices. An alderman does not think he is so far out of the way in selling his vote when he knows there are fifteen or twenty others who have gone at the same price. The clerk steals, and the cashier and his assistant conspire and embezzle, and the treasurer runs off with all the convertible assets of the corporation, with small compunction because so many others before them have betrayed the same trusts and committed the same offenses. Demonstrate that a majority of some legislature has been smirched with bribery, and the most corrupt of them all will hold his head as high as the cleanest gentleman in the land. Why do merchants adulterate their goods with so little sense of dishonesty and shame? Because so many do it. Why is the quality of so many articles which are offered for sale misrepresented to the customers? Because it is the habit of the trade. Ask a man, otherwise held to be decent and respectable, on what ground he justifies the carrying on of elections by tricks and frauds and lies, and his ready reply will be that candidates for office are not expected to be over-scrupulous. There is no sense of guilt. It is because men lump themselves in with the mass, and foster the notion that somehow the criminality of a bad act decreases just in the ratio of the increase of the number who are concerned in committing the bad act.

But this individuality of interest with which God regards men follows them along all these paths of vice and crime and down into all their depths of degradation. There may be ten or a thousand or a million who plot evil together and who join hands in villainy and injustice; but God's eye is on each of the entire company, and each in His view is singled out from all the rest. He follows each, and notes every evil thought and every wrong step and every bit of crookedness to which head and hand are lent. A hundred men with masked faces and the spirit of blackness in their hearts may be engaged in hanging a Negro to the limb of a tree or the beam of a bridge in Mississippi or Ohio, but each is none the less a murderer. Go where he will the brand of Cain is on his forehead.

IV.   *The same view is greatly serviceable when we contemplate the disappointments and sorrows and bitter experiences which fall to our lot.*

When we think of these disappointments and sorrows and bitter experiences as coming right from God to us individually, we are much more likely to learn the lessons they are meant to teach.

Here again we ward off the thought, and so defeat very often the purpose of our heavenly Father, by massing ourselves with the great body of our fellows. We say that sooner or later suffering is sure to come to all, and that we are under a common dispensation of general laws which take no note of individuals and make no exception in anybody's favor. The mother says: "Yes, I have lost my child; and my heart is wrung to agony; but how many mothers there are everywhere weeping for their little ones because they are not!" The son or the daughter says: "Yes, my mother is dead, and life is not now and never can be again what it was once, — what it was when morning by morning her face beamed upon me and her voice was music; but how many there are suffering from a like bereavement!" Or there is an accident, a railway collision, a drowning, a falling from a scaffold, a plunge to death down the shaft of an elevator, a premature discharge of a gun, a run-away; and it is all grouped under the head of natural causes or the chances to which all are subject. There is no effort to go behind the element of nature and see what the divine intent may be for us and how it may become a matter intensely personal to our souls. We miss the meaning of it and we miss the blessing of it, for the reason that we choose to think of ourselves as belonging to a great and indistinguishable multitude called humanity or as having our place in a system which is under the control of inexorable laws, and not as individuals, distinct from all others, and in whom God takes a distinct personal interest.

Our Lord took great pains to impress this view of the individualizing of God's regard for human souls in His teaching. Not a sparrow falls without the Father's notice; and the hairs of men's heads are numbered. If we are called upon to endure losses; if we are checked here and there with disappointments; if it is defeat to-day and still another defeat to-morrow; if it is blackness in the sky from year to year and life seems all overclouded with storms, — we may be sure there is a purpose in it for *us*. He took the babe out of the mother's arms, not only with a view to the highest good of the child, but also that He might teach the mother some lesson in the higher tuitions of life. He took the mother from the open fellowship of sons and daughters, not because He willingly afflicts and not alone because the mother was ripe for the heavenly ingathering, but that He might through the chastening and sanctifying influence of tears and the uplift of holy memories purify the hearts of those left behind. God, let it be said again, individualizes us. His interest in us is

direct and personal. If our property is swept away
by the flames or our earthly hopes are crushed or
death breaks our circles, it is that there may be
clearer vision of heavenly realities and a closer walk
with Christ.

> The hour of anguish passes by;
> But in the spirit there remains
> The outgrowth of the agony,
> The compensation of its pain,
> In meekness, which suspects no wrong,
> In patience, which endures control,
> In faith, which makes the spirit strong,
> In peace and purity of soul.

In general, then, it may be said that this thought
of the way in which God individualizes His regard
for us is one to give us much comfort and strength in
our Christian lives. We are not lost in the mass.
We are not overlooked in the multitude. A man
may fill but a very small place in this great, busy,
bustling world, and only a few may know him; but
God's regard goes out to him and enfolds him. A
man may seem to himself to be very unworthy of the
divine thought, and in reality be very much more
unworthy than he even seems to himself to be; but
not on this account is he excluded from this individualized interest of God. A man may be full of heart-
ache and sore burdened with care, and cup after cup
of secret sorrow may be pressed to his lips; but he
never has a need nor a pang which escapes God's
eye, — a need nor a pang which does not draw out
God's sympathy. "Who loved *me* and gave Himself for *me*."

Of any one who can say this as Paul said it, it is as Keble sings:

Thou art as much His care as if besides
Nor man nor angel lived in heaven or earth;
Thus sunbeams pour alike their glorious tide
To light up worlds, or wake an insect's mirth;
They shine and shine with unexhausted store.
Thou art thy Saviour's choice — seek no more.

BRINGING MEN TO GOD.

Because Christ also suffered for sins once, the righteous for
the unrighteous, that He might bring us to God.
1 Peter 3: 18.

OUR thoughts this morning are to gather about the
very practical and pressing matter of *Bringing Men
to God.*

That it is the supreme business of the church of
Christ to do the work of Christ will be generally conceded. "Follow Me" is an injunction which applies
not alone to individual believers, but to bodies of believers in their organized capacity. It applies also
to individual believers and to bodies of believers, not
only as respects their personal faith and their common creeds, but as respects all their aims and activities. Just what Christ would do if He were here
once more — a visible presence, possessing all the influence and all the power of the church and with all
the opportunities open to Him which are open to the
church for molding the thought and life of the
world — the church itself ought to do.

What the work of Christ is the words before us
make clear. He who is at once the great teacher
and the divine Redeemer was here upon the earth
to bring men to God. That was the outlook and

256

sweep of His intent. He became incarnate; He spoke His word; He wrought His deed; He suffered in the garden and on the cross; He went down into the grave, and rose again and ascended on high, where He ever liveth to make intercession for us, — in order to restore the broken loyalty of human hearts to the eternal and beneficent Father of us all.

This is the large and all-inclusive fact touching Christ, — the open secret of Bethlehem and Calvary. About other points there may be debate. This admits of no question. From first to last and all through, the eye of Christ was fixed steadily on the rescuing of men. This is His own explanation of His mission, — to reach and rescue men. He was here to pour light in on the minds of men, so that they could have some adequate understanding of truth and duty. He was here to break the fetters of men and lift their burdens of guilt from human hearts. He was here to open a path along which the weary, wandering feet of men might walk into light and blessedness. He was here to restore to men their lost communion with God and to make divine things real and precious to the soul. If a man believed Christ and followed Christ, that, in every instance, was what came of it, — he found himself brought to God.

With a distinctness and an emphasis not to be misunderstood, precisely this is declared in the passage in hand: "Because Christ also suffered for sins once, the righteous for the unrighteous, *that He might bring us to God.*"

This being true, and so evident withal as to shut
out the need of any discussion, the stress of interrogation falls on ways and means. How may this
work of bringing men to God be done? With what
sort of arguments, in what sort of temper, through
what agencies, methods, appliances may believers
and bodies of believers hope to be most successful
in taking up and carrying on to ultimate completeness that which our Lord began and for which He
lived and died?

Proceeding at once to the task of answering the
questions—and especially the main question—here
propounded, I have no hesitation in saying that

I. *First of all there must be a profound recogni-*
tion and a faithful use of the facts and truths which
were present to the mind of Jesus, and which moved
Him in His divine mission.

Sitting at His feet to learn what was the central
and all-embracing aim of Jesus, we must also sit at
His feet to learn what facts He carried along, and
what truths He wielded to accomplish His aim. It
will not do to overlook any truth which He considered
significant. It will not do to pronounce lightly any
truth on which He laid accent. It will not do to
magnify truths which, as He seems to have judged,
can play but little part in the great redemptive process of winning and purifying and upbuilding souls.
It will not do to marshal truths in such an order that
what He placed first is last, and what He put last is
first. We are to look at the work to be done from

His standpoint and to move forward under His guidance. Jesus knew the Father; He knew Himself; He knew the ages past; He knew the ages to come; He knew the moral and spiritual condition of humanity; He knew the nature and the perils and the possibilities of all souls; and knowing all, He knew exactly what was needed to bring men into accord with God. What was needed He used. It would be a strange conceit to suppose that the Son of God made mistakes, or that He did not know what considerations to press as being best adapted to secure His divine ends. It would be an equally strange conceit, and one altogether out of joint with any theory possible to be held of the Son of God as a Saviour for all men, in all lands and in all ages, to suppose that there has been any such change in the essential elements of human nature or in modern environments, that the facts on which He based His appeals and the truths He urged are now and henceforth antiquated and inapplicable.

As the Gospels open themselves to my apprehension, and the recorded career of Him who was the Light of the world, and who spake as never man spake becomes luminous and distinct, there are several large facts which appear and reappear. These facts seem to have been always latent in the thought of Jesus. They dominated His teaching. He used them continually, sometimes in one form and sometimes in another, as occasion required, and with this pressed to the front to-day and that to-morrow, to show men their true relation to God and their future prospect under the sweep of violated law and their value in the Divine estimation and their possibilities through the exercise of faith and repentance, and to persuade them to turn from folly and sin and become the children, sweet and loving and loyal, of the Father.

What are these facts?

I.   *To begin with, this sad and awful one that men are away from God.*

This fact underlies all. Jesus Christ came into the world to bring men to God, because men had wandered off into alienation and distance from God. In heart and life they were away from God. Jesus never lost sight of this fact. He never permitted his heart to escape the burden and pressure of it. Whether directly asserted on all occasions or not, man's lost condition was always and everywhere present to His thought, the assumption on which His life and His word and His death proceeded. He saw men away from God in the sense that they were morally and spiritually blind, and did not know how nor where to find Him. He saw men away from God in the sense that they were disinclined to find Him, and were doing what they could to shut the knowledge and will of God out of their minds. He saw men away from God in the deeper sense still that they had broken the Divine law, and were under condemnation, with no power, save through the interposed grace of God, to escape punishment; and with no time nor place for the momentous transaction save the here

and the now.   If men claimed to be in accord with
God, Jesus held up before them the Divine standards
touching faith and love and prayer and patience and
purity and obedience, and showed what were the inward and outward reaches of these requirements.
Or He pointed out to them their unbeliefs and their
inconsistencies and delinquencies and gross corruptions, and they were quite sure to retreat abashed.
Even in the best, like the young man who had kept
the commandments, and Nicodemus, so thoughtful
and circumspect and reputable, there was some lack
which indicated more than a mere surface dishar-
mony with God. The eye of Jesus swept the circuit;
He took in those of high degree, and those of low,
men of culture, men of wealth, men unlettered and
simple, men of position and power; but what He saw
everywhere was men away from God.   He saw men
poor and deaf and blind and miserable; He saw them
disheartened and faint and worn and weary; He saw
them in bonds to evil passions and lusts, smiting and
crowding each other, dead to righteousness, alive to
iniquity; but it was all reducible to this one formulary:
Away from God.

Jesus felt this.   It was a burden on His soul and
in His speech. It sobbed into expression in His tears.
It imparted the tenderness of a Divine accent to His
invitations.   It lay behind all His pangs and agonies
that men are at vast and dreary distances from God.

2.   *Notwithstanding their ill-desert and unworthi-
ness, God loves men, and yearns for their return to*

Him with the measureless interest of a divine affection.

Never has the love of God for men had such expression as in Jesus Christ. Never has the love of God for men had such appreciation and magnifying as by Jesus Christ. It was atmosphere to His life. It informed His thought. It constrained His action. It illuminated His speech. It overarched all His moods like a resplendent firmament. It was the ground on which He stood when He would give heart and hope to men, and lift them up into self-respect and a realization of their possibilities. Men are away from God in alienation and sin; but God loves them, loves them compassionately, loves them graciously, loves them with all the wealth and warmth of the great, infinite Heart.

Men sometimes think of the love of God as articulating itself in the murmur of brooks and the grace and sweetness of flowers and the softness of glowing skies and landscapes radiant with every form of beauty; and they say: "Look up and look abroad and see how the regard of God for His creatures ripples out into smiles over all the face of nature." Or they advance from this mere sentimentalism to the thought of that general goodness by which we have been made capable of happiness, and through which, in our own individual hearts and in our homes and in our social life, we receive so many tokens of the divine interest in our welfare and enjoyment. But to what heights above, to what depths below all this reaches the thought of Jesus! "For God so loved the world that He gave His only begotten Son, that whosoever believeth in Him should not perish, but have everlasting life. For God sent not His Son into the world to judge the world; but that the world should be saved through Him." That is love. For it is love for men, not because they are sweet and lovable and may fitly be approved by adding to their joy, but because they are so far out of the way, and so much need love, and only through the extended hand and the patience and the brooding care and the sanctifying grace of love can be made sweet and lovable.

With what unwearied repetition and through what a variety of memorable parables Jesus exalted and pressed that thought! Men might be as lost bits of coin, but they were precious still and there was One who would search for them and find them, if possible. Men might be as lost sheep, but there was One who would wind His way through the dark ravines and climb the mountain slopes and bring them back rejoicing, if only they would let Him. Men might be as prodigals, afar and degraded and miserable, but there was One who would watch for them and be sure to see them while yet a great way off, and run to meet them and give them joyful welcome on their return. Looked at in the grime and distortion of their sinfulness, it might seem impossible for God to love men. But Christ stood in the presence of all sorts of defilement and said: "God loves still." That is the climax and glory of love.

3. *It is only through Jesus Christ that men away from God in the alienation of sin find their way back to God.*

"I am the Way and the Truth and the Life." "No man cometh unto the Father but by Me." "That whosoever believeth on Him should not perish."

It is possible and, as I think, needful, — needful because fidelity to the truth as it is in Jesus and the interests of an aggressive Christianity require it, — to go further and say that Jesus held forth the fact of salvation through Him on the ground that He came into the world to be an atoning vicarious sacrifice.

It is claimed in some quarters, and with a great deal of earnestness, that our Lord never associated the notion of sacrifice with His sufferings, but, on the contrary, seemed careful to avoid expressions which contained sacrificial allusions. The Gospels not only do not justify this, but they show the reverse to be the fact. Permitting Himself to be announced by the forerunner as "the Lamb of God, who taketh away the sin of the world," He set the seal to the announcement with His own declaration that "the Son of Man came not to be ministered unto, but to minister, and *to give His life a ransom for many.*" More and more as the end drew on, when all was to be consummated in the crucifixion, did Jesus force that thought on the attention of those about Him. Say nothing of passages in His discourse in the upper chamber, of His strange and otherwise unaccountable agony in the garden, — nothing of His conversation with the disciples after the resurrection; and take just simply the language employed by Jesus in the institution of the Supper, and see how it confirms what is here avowed of a sacrificial element in His teaching. As has been said, this was "the most important and solemn of all the occasions on which our Lord ever alluded to His death." In this instance "He did so in terms that are unequivocally sacrificial, bringing it into close comparison with the paschal sacrifice, speaking of His blood as shed for many for the remission of sins, and further styling it the blood of the new covenant, so as to assimilate it to that sacrificial blood with which the old covenant was ratified and inaugurated. Indeed, of all the testimony which has been borne to the doctrine of the atonement in any part of the sacred volume, this testimony which is conveyed in the Lord's Supper is the most important; because it not only exhibits the doctrine in the clearest light, but incorporates it with the highest exercise of religious worship and perpetuates the remembrance of it in a monumental rite, which is destined to continue throughout all ages until the end of the world."

These are the facts which Christ used. Men are away from God, but God loves them still. Men are away from God, and may come back to God; but it is only through the light and the atoning merit of Him "who suffered for sins once, the righteous for the unrighteous." There are no facts with which to displace these facts. There are no truths in advance of these truths.   There are no arguments which can do the work, in the long run, of these arguments. They are Christ's own arguments.

It is said not unfrequently of late that there is a new sense, a revived sense of the love of God abroad; and that men are returning to the views Jesus entertained of the compassion and sympathy of the Divine Father.   If so, well, and more than well.   But, unluckily, much of this talk as it falls on my ear shades off into a sentimental modification of the fact, on the one hand, that men are seriously and criminally away from God, and of the fact, on the other hand, that there is no escape from the guilt and pollution and dominion of sin save through faith in the crucified Christ.

If we echo the voice of Jesus we shall magnify the love of God; but in the illumination of it we shall see men not nearer to Him, but farther away in guilt, and we shall see Jesus with His pierced hands and His pierced side as the One, and the One only, who is able to save unto the uttermost all who come unto God by Him.

II.   *To be effective in bringing men to God, the spirit of Christ must be caught, and His method largely reproduced.*

Spirit and method are not one, they are distinct ideas; but the spirit of Jesus had so much to do in shaping His method, and His method was so illustrative of His spirit and so vital to the free outworking of it, that for general purposes the two may well be grouped together.

It is all summed up in the single sentence: He
went about doing good. That was the spirit that
was in Him: to do good; and His way was to do
good always and everywhere, as openings presented
themselves or could be made. There is a glimpse of
it in this single statement: "And Jesus went about
all Galilee, teaching in their synagogues and preaching the gospel of the kingdom and healing all manner of sickness and all manner of disease among the
people." It was doing good all abroad and in all
sorts of ways.

The central and most characteristic element in the
spirit of Jesus was self-sacrifice. This was the heart
within heart of His being. Originally in the form of
God, He did not think the privilege and glory of
equality with God something to be tenaciously clung
to, but He emptied Himself and took the form of a
servant. Love with Him was self-denial and self-
surrender, and He loved to the far point where love
is ready to give all and to bear all for the sake of
others. He was righteous, but He saw others unrighteous and helpless through their unrighteousness,
and He took His own righteousness and laid it down
as a bridge over which men, blind and crippled and
burdened with guilt, might walk into the peace and
blessedness of the divine kingdom. He was righteous, but He was willing to die, if through His death
a highway might be cast up for the return of the unrighteous to the favor of God. "The righteous for
the unrighteous, that He might bring us to God."

Out of this came the loving interest, the wealth of patience, the tender and touching persuasiveness which were in Him, and the readiness to go all lengths to overcome the prejudices of men, enlighten their ignorance and restore to them a sense of the sweetness of knowing and serving God. How He yearned for men! How easy and natural it was for Him to take His place beside men of all classes and in all conditions, and to assure them of sympathy in all their distresses and disabilities and needs!

The eccentricities of men did not disturb Him. He was not thrown out of poise because Zaccheus chose to run the risk of making himself ridiculous by climbing a tree in order to see Him as He passed. He was not afraid of being accused of boisterous fanaticism because poor blind Bartimeus, the wayside beggar, in the intensity of his zeal strode over all the proprieties and clamored like a madman for the mercy of the divine Healer. He was not alarmed lest somebody should speak in disparagement of His mission and call it small, if He chose to give gracious audience to the solicitous mothers and send them away with His benediction resting on the heads of the babes they bore in their arms. It did not embarrass Him at all that the woman to whom He said: "God is a spirit; and they that worship Him must worship in spirit and truth," was a disreputable woman. He did not start up and say: "Now I shall be misjudged by this Pharisee whose hospitality I am enjoying," when the woman who was a sinner brought her alabaster box of ointment with which to anoint His feet, and stood behind Him weeping. "They that be whole need not a physician." He was here to seek and to save that which was lost. Every pulsation of His divine heart was in line with that sublime purpose. The spirit of self-sacrifice was so absolute in Him and over Him, His interest in men was so deep and tender, that, no matter who it was nor where it was, He helped and saved if possible. Traditions, current methods of doing things, fears of misapprehension in the popular mind had no influence in keeping Him back from reaching men.

We fall often to discussing whether we may work in this way or that; whether it is dignified and orderly to go out on the green grass of the park and the commons and unoccupied lots, and stand at the street-corners, to herald the good news of salvation for all. The expediency of a measure, new or old, ordinary or extraordinary, is always an open question. Men have a right to ask concerning plans already adopted or plans suggested: "Are they prudent and promising?" But it sometimes looks as though it were a matter of serious doubt in the minds of not a few whether it is a proper thing to try to save souls unless they will consent to be saved inside the four walls of some dedicated and, quite likely, highly decorated meeting house. There are thousands and thousands of church-members in this land who really seem to think that they and the very decorous religion which they have espoused are somehow compromised by open-air preaching and evangelistic meetings and announcement of services in the newspapers and cards and circulars printed and scattered like autumn leaves, inviting and urging people to the house of prayer. It is not denied in so many words that it is a good thing to save people; but they must be saved at just such a time and at just such a place and in just such a way, and, unless it is done through the proxy of some subordinate missionary agency, they must be just such people,— very nice and clean and cultivated.

But Jesus never permitted considerations of this sort to have any weight with Him. If He could reach men He reached them. With Jesus the place was always suitable, and the men and women before Him, whatever might chance to be their class, were always suitable, if only there were ears attent to His words and souls hungry for the truth; and the best that was in Him was always given if men would only take it. Jesus never kept Himself for occasions, and He never held His choicest thoughts in reserve; but He poured out truth as fountains pour water for all athirst. The profoundest word ever spoken of worship was addressed by Jesus to one listener. Sunday or Monday, at high noon or midnight, in religious assembly or in the throng and stir of the market place or along the dusty thoroughfare or in the privacy of domestic retreats, in temples made with hands or out in the great temple whose dome is the sky and whose lights are the unquenchable stars, with many to hear or only few, that blessed word "come" was always on His lips, and it was so spoken that men with an ear to hear caught always the accent of a heavenly love.

It is only through this spirit of Christ, actuating us in all our methods and pushing us forward into His method of constant watchfulness and of direct and personal application of the truth as often as there is any promise of usefulness, that we shall be successful in bringing men into the faith of our Lord and under the power of an endless life. It takes a wisdom born of this spirit to bring men to God and make them His. There is a wisdom of statesmanship. There is a wisdom of buying and selling. There is a wisdom of managing mills. There is a wisdom of sailing ships. There is a wisdom of cultivating lands. There is a wisdom of building houses and bridges. There is a wisdom of conducting educational institutions and pushing forward moral reforms. There is a wisdom of sweet homes and of choice and elevating social circles. So there is a wisdom of bringing men to Him whose divine image we all bear and whose will it is our highest glory to follow. This wisdom consists in coming to such a degree under the constraining love of Christ and into such profound identification with Christ in His outreach after lost men, that it shall no longer seem to us a vast condescension to take our places beside men just as they are and lock hands with them in a helpful human fellowship. It will not be without cost. It was not without cost to Him, and it will not be without cost to us. Bringing men to God is not a May-game business. The kingdom of heaven is not to be ushered in with noise of rolling drums and the pomp of parade and flying banners, but only as somebody wrestles and toils and prays and loves. But while it is hard, and only possible through the spirit of Christ stirring our hearts and warming our hands and pressing us on, yet under the influence of this spirit men will yield and turn to God.

Herein lies the solution of the much-debated question of reaching the masses. That the church ought to reach the masses is beyond controversy. Think of them. Multitudes on multitudes, swaying back and forth, clutching at every kind of self-defense, driven hither and thither by all sorts of winds and cross-winds of doubts and queries and denials, without God and without hope in the world! Ministers, churches, associations, councils, conferences, congresses, clubs, seminaries ought to give themselves no pause till they have come to some satisfactory conclusion as to the best ways of getting the truth as it is in Jesus pressed on the attention of the masses. Those are words of deep significance which Professor Phelps addresses to ministers. But while especially applicable to ministers, they are applicable also to all who in any way co-work with ministers and share with them in the responsibility of acquainting all men with God. "A preacher had better work in the dark, with nothing but mother-wit, a quickened conscience and a Saxon Bible to teach him what to do and how to do it, than to vault into an aerial ministry in which only the upper classes shall know or care anything about him. You had better go and *talk* the gospel in the Cornish dialect to those miners who told the witnesses summoned by the committee of the English parliament that they had 'never heard of Mister Jesus Christ in these mines,' than to do the work of the bishop of London. Make your ministry reach the people; with elaborate doctrines, if possible, but reach the people; with classic speech, if it may be, but reach the people. The great problem of life to an educated ministry is to make their culture a power instead of a luxury. Our temptations are all one way; our mission is all the other way."

For one, I have no fancy for what are called Salvation Armies. They are not to my taste. But who am I, who are we, to interpose our criticisms and protests, if men are actually reached and taken out of the slums of all degradation and brought to God? I do not believe in being made the cat's-paw of shrewd land-speculators and wily catch-penny maneuverers, who pretend great zeal for religion and who thinly disguise their schemes by calling them camp-meetings. But it is absolutely certain that not a few find God in these gatherings. Are so many finding God in the ordinary and unobjectionable ways? Are so many trying to walk worthy of God that we can afford to say men shall not come in unless they come by gates having the true æsthetic design and proportion and finish? It is not to be forgotten that the city which John saw coming down out of heaven from God had twelve gates: "On the east three gates; on the north three gates; on the south three gates; and on the west three gates." If those northern gates were for cool, circumspect people, quite likely the southern are for impetuous, shouting folk like Bartimeus. If wild "mountain evangelists" and if "boy preachers" with their extravagances and contortions can only succeed in bringing men to God, it is not for anybody to rise up and forbid them.

At the same time, if the spirit and method of Christ could only be reproduced in the disciples of Christ, and men and women of culture and wealth and influence, with characters unimpeached and positions assured, could be induced to let the love of Christ flow out through them, putting a look of compassion into the eye and a tone of tenderness into the voice and a sympathetic warmth into the hand, it would go further than all the schemes and devices which can be hatched in a thousand years toward settling this whole problem of reaching the masses. There is not a church in America so stiff and cold that it could not be popularized in a twelvemonth if only the ten or twelve leading members, men and women, would set themselves to the task in the spirit and after the method of Christ. The trouble is that all our tendencies and inclinations are toward the top. Worldly

methods and habits of estimating men hold us in
their grip. Our standards are commercial and social
and æsthetic. Ambition and pride and love of ease
displace the spirit of self-sacrificing service. The
gravitations on the human side are upwards and towards exclusiveness. Churches are like pines; when
they begin to grow their limbs are low down, and
the little timid birds may perch in their branches,
and find shelter and sing their songs. But as they
stretch up, year by year, their lower limbs fall off,
until at last their tops are so high that there is only
housing in them for the eagles and the hawks and
the crows. The poor timid groundlings must look
elsewhere, and the distrust is spread all abroad. The
correction of the mischief lies not in inventing machinery which will have more clatter when in motion than
the simple church of Christ, nor in running off into
what may be called church-annexes of one sort and
another; but in taking up into ourselves, and illus-
trating in all our comings and goings, the spirit which
was in Him. That spirit in the pulpit and in the
pews will reach the masses and bring men to God.

III. *Our conception of what it is to bring men to
God must be as large and all-inclusive as was the conception of Jesus.*

With Jesus this work took two forms and involved
two processes. The one was what we technically
call the conversion of men, and the other was the
building up of men in righteousness. The one was
inducing men to recognize God, to have faith in

Him and in the spirit of loving submission to His will to turn about from their old bad ways and walk in His paths; the other was making them like God, — sweet, affectionate, helpful and grandly loyal to every truth and duty. He said "Believe," and He led just as many as possible to the exercise of faith and repentance; but He never stopped there. He took believers right on — insisted that they themselves should go right on — into the doing of the divine will, and so forming character.

It is unfortunate for the interest of the church, or rather for the interest of humanity, whose regeneration the church under God aspires to accomplish, that this twofold notion has not always been kept in mind. Some have seemed to maintain that conversion is the chief business and that when men have been made thoughtful, anxious, led into the inquiry-room, brought to their knees in confession and supplication, persuaded to bear testimony to the grace of God shed abroad in their hearts in some public way and to unite in membership with believers, they may be dismissed from care. Others have seemed to maintain that this preliminary work of winning men into the faith and acknowledgment of God is of little consequence in comparison with instructing and establishing them in the principles of the new life. Whereas, the true conception takes in both these ideas. Men are to be won to the faith, and then they are to be built up in the faith. It is not one or the other; it is not one over against the other; it is one and the other.

Paul, better than any other, perhaps, interprets for us the breadth and sweep of Christ's conception of bringing men to God. If we look for the unifying element in the life and teaching of the great apostle, we find it in his complete and uncompromising devotion to Christ. This was his absorbing passion. But the service which was the outgrowth and expression of his one thought of devotion took two directions, the winning and the upbuilding; and any man may well be challenged to tell in which Paul was the more interested.

Paul sought men, and he sought them with all the ardor and energy of his great soul. His desire to acquaint men with God in Christ, and to persuade them to accept Him, was a fire in his bones. He was as eager to catch men for the Lord as any fisherman ever was to hook trout or grayling or any sportsman to bag his game. He went from city to city, from province to province, from Asia across into Europe; he took advantage of the opportunities afforded him when he was summoned into the presence of governors and others in authority; he availed himself of disasters by sea and of persecutions by land; he pushed his way into the great centers of learning and trade and commerce; he condescended to the lowly; he toiled with his own hands; he suffered want; he endured reproach and abuse, — all that he might press Jesus and the resurrection on the attention of men. Unweariedly and everywhere he beckoned men to the Lord. He saw the great masses

of mankind astray and alienated from the life of God,
he saw souls everywhere defiled and bondaged and
burdened by sin, and the impulse took possession of
him and kept possession of him to go forth to the
rescue. It is but a blind and unsympathetic reading
of the life of Paul which finds nothing to awaken intense desire and to inspire intense activity in the direction of winning men into discipleship.

The mistake is in assuming that this exhausts the
meaning of Paul's life and covers all his work. He
had an after-care. His zeal for winning souls passed
over into zeal for developing and training souls. He
saw no place for pause short of complete conformity
to the pattern of Jesus. He aimed at pure and exalted character. He wanted men who believe to be
large and full and round in their manhood, informed
and vitalized with truth, able to stand erect in a
clean-handed righteousness, intelligent and just and
sweet in their lives. He urged to integrity. He
wanted men *to be* all that the confession of Christ
implies, to walk worthy of their high vocation. His
soul swelled with the impatience which is born of an
affectionate interest in the presence of those who
were content to stand still and be largely just what
they always had been. "Forward" was his watch-
word. Pressing himself toward the mark for the
prize of the high calling of God in Christ Jesus, he
desired others to do so too. His prayer in behalf of
the Ephesians was "that He would grant you, according to the riches of His glory, to be strengthened

with might by His Spirit in the inner man; that Christ
may dwell in your hearts by faith; that ye, being
rooted and grounded in love, may be able to comprehend with all saints what is the breadth and length and
depth and height, and to know the love of Christ,
which passeth knowledge, *that ye might be filled with
all the fullness of God.*" What a standard! What a definite and intense longing that believers may realize to
the full all that is made possible for them through the
revelation of God in Christ, and by their new birth into
the kingdom! *Unto a perfect man* was the goal he
fixed. It is impossible to read his letters without being made to feel this. His epistles are aglow with enthusiasm for the growth of believers in knowledge and
love and purity and moral strength, and every quality
which enters into our ideal of character.

There is a pertinent and very significant fact stated
in *Acts*. In the account of their first missionary
journey we read of a retracing of steps by Paul and
Barnabas. "They returned again to Lystra and to
Iconium and Antioch." In these second visits to the
cities they had once passed through, what were they
doing? "Confirming the souls of the disciples and
exhorting them to continue in the faith." The whole
aim was to establish and strengthen, to encourage
and to instruct disciples concerning the truth and
way of God. It was not enough that they had begun in Christ; they must be built up in Christ. As
yet they were only beginners; they must go on.
They were babes; they must become men. Their

faith must be carried forward and crystallized into robust character.

Great stress, then, is laid on the winning of men; but stress just as great is to be laid on building them up. They are to be won with a view to building them up, and built up because the winning is abortive without it. It would be an unpardonable offense to reduce Christianity to a mere educating force, or to drop down into the notion that the kingdom of our Lord is to be advanced till it fills and dominates the earth just by training those who already believe or who from time to time may chance to find their way into the faith. But it is an offense of no less magnitude to gather men in and then leave them unripe and undeveloped, not broad and intelligent and integral and alive in every power and faculty with the life of God, but narrow and one-sided. Men are not brought to God in anything more than a mere rudimentary way until they are brought in the amplitude and fullness which lift their whole being into the light, and project them in all their thoughts and aims and activities along the line of the divine will.

This means men of large faith, men of purity, men of fidelity, men who are open and straightforward, men who will not lie nor cheat nor steal nor meanly equivocate; men whose virtue will not melt away under the seductions of pleasure nor the temptations of bribes; men whose pulse is warm and strong with love and whose hands are quick to help; men with intelligent convictions in their souls and who walk their ways and do their work in the confidence that obeying conscience and following God are never without exceeding great rewards.

Remembering the thief on the cross, and what our Lord said to him, I do not dare to ridicule the assurances sometimes expressed by condemned criminals about to be executed that they are going straight from the hangman's hands into glory. But I am very certain the religion we want, and the religion we shall have when men have been brought to God in the large way of Christ's conception, will be a religion which will not do so much to enable men to go up singing and shouting from the gallows as to keep them from the gallows.

No organization can escape the annoyance and discredit of pretenders. The purer any association may be, the more surely will it be used by designing men and arrant hypocrites. Still, there are too many who bear the Christian name to be found in our state-prisons and penitentiaries. Or if they have not reached these lengths in crime and exposure and punishment, there are too many whose word is not good, whose fidelity is not equal to the strain of a large trust, who fall too easily into all the tricks and duplicities of the world and whose general honesty needs the sharp tonic of a daily watch. "Lord, who shall abide in Thy tabernacle? He that walketh uprightly and worketh righteousness and speaketh the truth in his heart." When men are brought to God, or when they come to God in the right way, it is in the totality of themselves, — head, hand, heart; and these for every day in the week and for every place under the canopy of heaven. To bring men to God in the right way, and in the completeness of the bringing, is to bring their homes along with them and their schools and their stores and their factories and their counting-houses and their politics and their laws and customs and institutions and their newspapers and their literature and their wealth and their special gifts of genius, sweetening all, elevating and broadening all and writing across the whole economy of life: "Holiness unto the Lord."

THE INCREASING CHRIST.

He must increase. John 3: 30.

THESE are the words of John the Baptist. They were uttered when his own mission was nearly accomplished, and when the great work of Jesus on earth was just commencing. Finding in them a theme always quickening, it has seemed to me good to devote the time put at my disposal to a reverent and earnest consideration of *The Increasing Christ*.

Doing so it will be my endeavor to show that this prediction of the Forerunner has abundant justification in the position which our Lord actually holds among men to-day.

I. *Naturally our first inquiry will concern the relation of Jesus to the brain of the time, or the estimate which is put upon Him by the instructed and sober judgment of the age.*

In the conception of many, this, in addition to being logically the true point of departure for such a discussion, is the most vital test that can be applied, while there is no one who will not regard it as of great consequence to be determined. For the ideas of men, the opinions which they intelligently form, the sentiments which they inwardly cherish, will sooner or later crystallize into fact and control life. The real thoughts of to-day, whether announced or not, are the grooves along which will run the customs and institutions and creeds of to-morrow. The latent convictions which are entertained after men have patiently studied and reflected are buds which will blossom sometime and become fruit. If there be anything which has ceased to have entrenchment in the enlightened thought of the world, its complete overthrow is only a matter of time. If there be anything that is becoming more and more buttressed with the growing assent of cultivated intelligence, no concern need be felt for its future.

He whom we regard as the Saviour of the world and at whose feet millions fall in devoutest adoration and trust, can not in the long run be an exception to the rule. Before the bar of that calm reason in the soul of man to which God Himself, through the mouth of the prophet, has seen fit to make appeal, He must take His place.

How fares it, then, with Jesus in the schools? What do instructed and strong men think about Him? Looking back at Him across the space of eighteen centuries and from the illuminated heights of our modern learning, as He lies there in the manger at Bethlehem or hangs on the cross of Calvary, and taking His words and His works and His character and bringing them into the focus of our latest and clearest light, what are the conclusions which competent men are forced to draw? Has criticism taken Him down from His high place in the world of thought and broken his grasp on the judgment of large and sincere minds? Or in the opinion of the best informed and most candid is He still able to maintain His hold as the true Son of God?

Fortunately we are not without materials on which to base an answer. Never before has there been a time when it was possible to approach the matter with so many and so varied results of investigation, and when there was such a volume of experience and testimony of one kind and another actually on record to help in arriving at trustworthy conclusions. For eighteen hundred years the story of Jesus has been before the world; and it has led to numberless speculations and controversies. The questions of His nature, His doctrines, the ends at which He aimed and of the need and merits of His death have all been examined and re-examined, until the books which contain the outcome of these labors are an immense library by themselves. But at no previous period have men been so intent on getting at the exact facts of His human history and knowing precisely what He said and did and was, as within the last fifty years. He, indeed, is the pivot over which the profoundest thought of the age has played. He is the problem on which the highest scholarship of our generation has been concentrated. To estimate and locate Him beyond the necessity of any re-adjustment of His claims has been the task the most earnest and scholarly intellects in the religious world have assigned to themselves, and which the awaiting masses have demanded should be accomplished. He has been felt to be the key-position in the conflict; and both assailants and defenders have concentrated their heaviest forces on Him, as though it were mutually understood that if He can be carried then all can be carried, and if He can be held then all can be saved. Faith and philosophy alike have consented to join in this one common request: Tell us something — something sure and final, if it may be, about Jesus of Nazareth.

In this way it has come about that everything pertaining to the God-Man has been severely canvassed. The whole ground has been traversed and re-traversed. Both sides have investigated every minutest fact touching His birth and life and death and resurrection. Not only have believers sought Him out and studied His sayings and doings with an absorbing interest, but unbelievers as well, spurred on by a rashness which was barbed with hate, have invaded the circle of His being and dealt with Him as demonstrators in anatomy deal with a subject on the dissecting-table. Catching the spirit of a time when wonderful advances have been made all along the line of knowledge, and which is characterized by the overturning of old methods and the persistent re-investigation of facts and theories in all spheres, men have not hesitated to put the Divine One in their balances and weigh Him. His own questions were: " *Whom do men say that I am?*" and " *What think ye of Christ?*" These questions have been taken fearlessly up; the Gospel narratives have been sifted; and answers have been rendered. There has been no evasion of what was difficult and delicate. Nothing has been spared to prejudice. No statement, no atom of evidence, has been permitted to pass unchallenged and without the closest and most uncompromising scrutiny into its worth and bearing. However it may have been in other days, in these days there has been no holding back of conclusions lest the feelings of good souls might be shocked and the faith of trusting souls unsettled. More than this. There have been men, not a few, who seemed to take delight in reviving the council of the Jews and bringing in their predetermined verdict of guilty. Or in repeating the demand of the excited mob and crying: Crucify Him! Crucify Him! Or in re-enacting the cruelty of the soldiers and thrusting the spear-point of their sharpest malice into His side. If Christ be not the Christ and the world still insists on believing in His name, it is not because adequate effort has not been made to disabuse the nations of their confidence.

But we do not need to pass all these critical assaults and vindications in review. It so happens that in a large and comprehensive survey undertaken for the purpose of finding out the real standing of Jesus in the world of thought, there is one name which is conspicuous and significant above all others. In the attempt which this man made to overturn and destroy Jesus as though he were another Dagon set up in another temple of blind superstition, and in the reception which this effort met at the court of a wise

and sober public opinion, we have a fact which registers for us better than anything else to which we
can turn, the estimate in which the Son of God is
held throughout Christendom.

It is now sixty years since Strauss issued his famous *Life of Jesus*. This book startled like a clap
of thunder out of a clear sky. Coming from a land
already noted for its enthusiasm and eminence in
historic research and from the pen of one who,
though young when he wrote it, as Calvin was young
when he wrote his *Institutes*, each being only
twenty-seven years of age, was yet a scholar well
disciplined, of large resources, of indefatigable spirit
and of much promise, it compelled attention and
forced men to meet the issue of Christ or No-Christ,
fair and square.

When looked into, the book was found to be an
attempt to show that the Gospels as historic materials
cannot be trusted; that miracles are impossible; and
that Jesus Himself is only a myth.

It was on the latter proposition that chief stress
was laid; for it was the object of the work to reduce
Jesus to the rank of a divinity in the old heathen my-
thology. The real Jesus was not the Jesus of the
Gospels and of our Christian faith, but a person on
whom the imagination of men seized and dwelt until
he was exalted into a supernatural being.

These statements were supported by the canons of
what was claimed to be highest criticism and by the
inductions of what was claimed to be the most ad-

vanced science and by the dogmas of what was claimed to be the profoundest philosophy. It was the most studied and determined endeavor ever made to dislodge Jesus from His entrenchment in the intellectual regard of men. Fresh from the school of Baur with his vast wealth of knowledge and his iconoclastic spirit, a pupil also of Schleiermacher and steeped through and through with the philosophy of Hegel, he was able to bring the most polished weapons of wit and learning and logic to the encounter. In audacity and skill and thoroughness the centuries furnish no mate to this attack of Strauss on Jesus. Celsus aimed to do the same thing at an early day, but he was coarse in comparison and his arraignment consisted largely, as another has said, of a reproduction and endorsement of the motives of "Judaism with its unfulfilled ideas of the Messiah and its calumnious traditions." Later, Renan tried his hand in the same direction, but there is no such dead earnestness in his assault. On the contrary his *Life of Jesus* makes the impression of one who is simply playing with his subject, and is chiefly interested in what is romantic and beautiful about it. The German couched his lance for a straight heart-thrust. It was an assault upon the foundations. Whatever else it might leave us, it was designed to remove Him in whom we trusted for the delivery of the world from the guilt and pollution of sin.

What came of it? Did reason bend down in acquiescence? Did he carry with him the ripe intelligence of these latest years? Did instructed men give assent to this new theory as they did to the announcement of the law of gravitation?

The answers to these questions are open to the world. The radical position taken by Strauss and the arguments brought forward by him in support of his position set the scholars of the time upon an earnest re-investigation of the whole subject of Christ, His nature and character and place in humanity and the ground on which His claims rest. Not in all the centuries before were so many minds set upon the task of a severe critical examination of the record and secret of the power of our Lord, as undertook this work subsequent to the appearance of Strauss' *Life of Jesus*. From that day to this men distinguished for learning as well as piety have been pouring out their maturest conclusions on Christ and the authenticity and genuineness of the Gospel in which His wonderful story is told. It would take pages to recite the titles of the books on Christ which have been prepared by eminent authors and sent out into the world within the latter half of this century.

But the fact of significance is that these treatises on Christ which have been most loyal to the New Testament account of Christ are those which have won the deepest convictions and secured the widest approval among men. From an intellectual point of view Christ lost nothing, but gained much, through the assault of Strauss.

This, Strauss himself was forced to admit. For

after waiting about thirty years and devoting his energies to a wide range of studies, he re-appeared upon the stage with further statements concerning Christ. These statements were designed by him to be a summing up of the results of the combined criticisms of the world and to see what place the despised Nazarene still maintained in the minds of men after an attempt so ingenious and well organized and persistent to overthrow Him. The fruits of such an attempt might well have been looked for. If there was to be a marked change in religious opinion and men were to abandon Jesus, it might be expected that evidence of this would appear at the end of three decades. But, strange to say, according to his own frank admission, after all the examination of original material to which his attack had led and with so much time for the lesson of this new view to work and with a free press multiplying and a hundred-handed enterprise distributing his conclusions, not a solitary man eminent for ability and scholarship could be found either in Germany or France or England or America to go along with him in his conception of Christ.

Aristotle said that science, to be science, must be capable of being taught. This was the test he applied: Facts must be combined and phenomena explained in such a way as to certify themselves to the intelligence and candor of whoever might examine them.

Here was a disposition of ancient records and

a re-casting of well-settled opinions and ideas after a method which purported to be scientific; and yet nobody of commanding influence was ready to admit himself convinced that the old way of looking at Jesus was wrong and the new way right.

Strauss made partial converts. Some agreed with him in one thing, some in another. One would assent to his ruling out of certain portions of the Gospel. Another was ready to say miracles are impossible. But from the sheer abyss of a completely annihilated Jesus, as a merely mythical Jesus would be, all the leading thinkers turned back. Even Theodore Parker rebelled against the assumption that He whom this critic conceded to have been a "beautiful nature" and who was admitted to stand "foremost among those who have given a higher ideal to humanity" could have been evolved out of the mind of the age in which He had His birth.

Our question, therefore, is answered. The simple recitation of facts puts the whole case before us. Jesus Christ, through all investigations and under all assaults, has gained steadily on the sober, instructed judgment of mankind.

There is much out-and-out infidelity abroad. There are many conceptions of Christ and His work which are imperfect. There is, as there has always been and perhaps always will be, not a little impatience with attempts to reduce Christ to the measure of a creed. But men believe in Jesus; believe in Him in increasing numbers and with an increasing confidence. For the tide of thoughtful assent to His claims swells continually. Pride and opposition assail; but like the mountain-oak, smitten by storms, He only strikes His roots the deeper down into enlightened convictions. Assaults on Him only serve to clear the atmosphere of doubts, and make it seem more reasonable to accept and follow Him.

If it be said that the conception which we have of Jesus is a thing of gradual growth, men straightway ask: How explain the record of His life, a record complete and full from the outset, as the Gospels make evident beyond all gainsaying? If it be said that He was a deceiver, taking advantage of the expectation of His race and the credulity of His times to foist Himself on the world as the promised Messiah, men straightway point to His life and character and refuse to admit that such justice and holiness as He exhibited could have any association with hypocrisy. If it be said that He was an enthusiast, borne on by the heat of His own imagination, men straightway answer that there were a sobriety in His nature, a self-poise manifested in all His conduct and in all the ordeals through which He passed and especially a clear and accurate pre-vision of what was to come in succeeding ages as the result of His teaching and His death, wholly unaccountable on the basis of this conjecture and wholly irreconcilable with the world's notion of fanaticism.

These conceits and theories can make no general progress. Thoughtful men rebel against them. The realm of mind over which Jesus holds dominion does not lessen. It widens and widens. Looked at from the standpoint of a disciplined intelligence, Jesus is seen to be the Rock of Ages, and men build on Him and count it rational. He is seen to be the light of the world, and men walk in the radiance of His truth and know it is wise. He is seen to be the divine Helper, and men take His hand and under His leading find their way into the Father's house.

It is not the heart merely which has clung to Jesus and stoutly refused to give Him up; but the head has bowed down to the sublime miracle of His being, and reason has said and is saying still with an emphasis which never before marked her utterances on this great fact: "Truly this Man was the Son of God." Slowly but surely He is pressing on to the conquest of thought; and century by century, the world over, increasing numbers are joining in the confession of Peter: "And we have believed and know that Thou art the Holy One of God." No matter what theories are propounded nor what forms criticism takes, if they tend to diminish aught of the glory of Jesus, men put them away. All the great signs in the nations point to a time when not the masses simply, nor the representatives of the masses, but the master-minds also shall rise up and exclaim with Thomas: "*My Lord and my God!*"

II. *Observe, now, in the second place, the relation which Christ sustains to the hand or the power of the earth.*

In looking abroad, we find the total population of the globe to be something near 1,500,000,000. According to the latest estimates, these numbers are distributed as follows: To Australia and Oceania about 5,000,000; to America, about 130,000,000; to Africa, about 140,000,000; to Europe, a little over 380,000,000; and to Asia, not far from 850,000,000. Recent statistical writers have taken the ground, for reasons given, that the census of the East is vastly exaggerated, and that in China, for instance, there are not more than 200,000,000 of people, whereas the figures ordinarily set down are 400,000,-000.

But for the purposes now in view this makes no important difference. By any calculation it will be seen that more than two-thirds of the inhabitants of the earth are in Asia and Africa; and are still under the sway and within the realm of pagan influences. Many millions of these are in the depths of barbarism. If it is to be settled by majorities, Christ is very far from being the Master of the nations. Those who are in pagan countries are two to one, possibly three to one, against those who are nominally Christians. This shows a prodigious work yet to be accomplished by missionary enterprise.

Yet is it not a long stride onward — an immense increase in numerical strength, when a third or even a quarter of the whole human race has been made familiar with the name of Jesus and is wont to bend with a reverence more or less intelligent and sincere at the mention of Calvary?

Numbers, however, afford us only a rude idea of power, and actual strength has often to be sought by other methods than numerical comparisons. It certainly is so here. For when the nearly 1,000,000,-000 of Asia and Africa are weighed in the balance with the 500,000,000 of Europe and America, with the intent to ascertain where the more force resides, it is the larger number which quickly kicks the beam. Africa is bending under the burden of an ancient babarism, and Asia, until recently she has consented to open her life to new impulses from abroad, has been at a stand-still for centuries upon centuries; while the enterprise and energy of the earth are with the Western nations. Are ships to be sent out to whiten all the seas; are railroads to be built to link states and kingdoms together and to bring distant towns and cities into close proximity and to facilitate trade and social intercourse; are telegraphs to be constructed to flash thought afar and to aid the ends of the earth in coming into easy communication; are many inventions to be sought out and sciences to be pushed into unheard of applications and the methods of household toil and the implements of husbandry and the mechanic arts to be improved; are systematic efforts to be put forth through schools and books and newspapers and laws and social intercourse and home life and religion, to realize the best possibilities in the individual and in the state;—it is not the dead East, but the living West out of which the wondrous vitality necessary for the doing of these things must spring. Men to set things in motion must have the inspiration of motion in their own souls. They can not quicken others until they themselves are alive. When the Hottentot has measured muscle with the Anglo-Saxon, the comparison ends.

Respect for the Chinese has been increasing in the last half-century; though it must be admitted that in the recent conflict between China and Japan enthusiasm for China was somewhat checked. On the whole, however, a better knowledge of the Middle Kingdom has shown us that there are many things in the habits and methods and institutions of that people not altogether bad. But in general the Asiatic is afraid of progress. He sticks to tradition and routine. He is nimble; his memory serves him wonderfully; but the originating and aggressive faculty is only small. Life amongst these Oriental people is almost an exact duplicate of what it was thousands of years ago. No leavening force is in them, and no molding force goes out of them.

The power of the earth, the real power, because it is a power which has its source in knowledge and is alive with moral purpose and means not to sit on from age to age with folded hands, but to do something, is with the nations of the West.

What, now, is the bearing of this particular fact on the matter in hand? Very important. For it is in these nations of the West that Christ is acknowledged in pre-eminent degree. His name has been carried into China and Japan. What has been done in these empires, especially in Japan, in the last decade, is both preparation and shining prophecy of what is to be done in the near future. Thousands in India have accepted Him. Whole islands have turned their faces to Calvary and received the law at the mouth of the crucified Son of God. His disciples almost join hands in a circle around Africa; and in a little while at the very heart of that old, sad continent, with its mighty rivers and its vast and beautiful lakes and its brooding mysteries, the banner of the cross is to be unfurled, and men and women are to witness freely amongst the multitudes of these barbarian tribes for Jesus. But it is the new and thrifty and aggressive nations which have taken Him up and adopted His faith and wrought His ideas into their laws and institutions and made His life a part of their life. Thus His potency is with those who themselves are most potent in shaping earthly destinies. Numbers in large preponderance are still against our Lord. When resolution is pitted against resolution; when skill is measured with skill; when enterprise is set over in opposition to enterprise; when power locks hands with power, then we find Jesus sitting in the very gate of authority and inspiring the brains and nerving the hands and moving the arms, which control the actions of the world.

There is still a closer view to be taken of this subject. Up to this point the thought has been upon what calls itself nominal Christendom. Western empires and peoples have been looked at under this one classification. No distinctions have been made between the great bodies of those who accept Christ as their common Redeemer. Catholics and Greeks and Protestants have all been included without discrimination.

There are, be it observed, very suggestive facts lurking within these distinctions, and we shall not be likely to have any fit conception of the closeness with which Christ comes to the seat of modern power, until we have made a further analysis of these nations and have discovered which of them it is that wields the scepter of widest influence. For it needs little illustration to show that our Lord's strongest hold is upon those people which have the firmest grasp on human affairs, and do most to shape the public policies and determine the general drift of the world. Or, to turn the thought about a little, those nations which have the most of Christ in them, which come nearest to Him in the acceptance of His truth and life, are the nations which are the mightiest in the earth.

Here, again, numbers seem to be against the Son of Man. For while there are not less than 100,000,-000 in the Greek church in Europe, and in the neighborhood of 200,000,000 of Catholics in Europe and America, there are only about 150,000,000 of Protestants all told. But what is the distribution of these Greek and Catholic elements? Under what national banners do we find these bodies preponderating?

Mark the answer. For it is one of the significant results of the conflicts which have taken place within the last thirty years, or the period during which the late Emperor William sat upon the throne, that the balance of power in the earth has passed out of Catholic hands. The decisive struggles between Prussia and Austria, and Germany and France, wrought this important change. Only a little while ago Austria and France had but to call to arms and all Europe trembled. To-day each of these nations is struggling to recover from humiliations and disasters which left them with little terror in their threats.

Nor is this the whole statement of the case. While Catholic countries have been going down, Protestant countries have been going up. It was said in Paris only a few years ago, by a distinguished Catholic preacher, himself a native of France, that Protestant nations were advancing all the time while Catholic nations were on the decline. He gave facts in proof, some of which have just been indicated, and another of which was the steady growth of the United States over against the hopeless condition of such Catholic nations as Spain. One risks nothing in affirming that the vitality and force of the period are with the Protestant nations. The energetic and progressive nations, the nations which hold in their hands the acknowledged sovereignty of the times, are the nations in which Christianity resides in its simplest and purest forms.

Russia, it may be said, is an exception. It is only partly so. While Russia is not Protestant, neither is it Catholic. Though the Greek and the Catholic creeds and methods of worship have much in common — a great deal more than the Greek and the Protestant unless High Church Episcopacy be an exception, and though the spirit of the Greek church is exclusive and bitter, and Russia keeps her doors closed against Protestant preaching and influence, yet she holds fast to some of the better ideas which are latent in all forms of Christianity, no matter how perverted and abused.

In speaking of the *Unity of Christian Belief* in his book on *Faith and Rationalism*, Professor Fisher, of Yale University, says: "Christ has held the central place in the Christian system from the beginning until now. His incarnation and atonement have been continually the objects of faith. The Nicene theology was the perfecting of a definition, not the introduction of a new opinion. That theology has been for substance the creed of Greek, Roman Catholic and Protestant, the only exception being sects which professed to dissent from the common belief." These cardinal facts have still a large place and power in the Greek church in Russia.

But even though there were nothing in this, Russia would still be only partly exceptional, for the reason that her influence on the outside world is not great. It is the Protestant nations which are most vigorous and most aggressive and most potential.

It is hardly a figure of speech, therefore, to say that in an emphatic sense the armies of the earth to-day are Christ's, that the commerce of the world is Christ's, that the most efficient wealth of the time is Christ's, that the laws which reach farthest and the thrones which cast the longest shadow and the public opinion which is the most commanding have on them, one and all, the sign-manual of our Lord. I know how imperfect the recognition of Christ is even among the most Christian people; what multitudes of exceptions can be cited to the universality of His rule; how worldliness dominates in the church, and how corruption runs riot in society, and how we have to hang our heads in shame every little while at the developments made concerning men and women thought to be pure; but is it not much — a vast increase in power over the world — for Jesus to hold a place so near as He now does to the very heart of universal control?

III. *Consider further the relation which Christ sustains to the heart of the world, or the influence He has come to have over the affections and conduct of men.*

Here we touch what is central and decisive. The dominion which Christ came to establish is a dominion of souls. In one sense it matters little that the brain of the earth is forced to acknowledge the validity of His claims, and that nations wield their authority and mold their institutions in less or more of allegiance to His truth, if He does not have a place and a growing place in the affectionate regards of men, and more and more of control over human actions.

Is Christ, then, working His way into hearts? Is His life becoming the informing principle in the lives of numbers ever growing larger and larger?

There are two directions in which we may look for answer; and the answers we shall find in these directions seem to me conclusive.

1. Following along in the line of the first sphere of inquiry, we are led to examine the matter of the personal attachment of believers to their Lord and to ask whether men love Him as they once did and whether the numbers of those who love Him are multiplying.

Nothing is more common than to make disparaging comparisons between the present and the past. Facts seen through the golden mists of long-gone times become exaggerated. We may be too near to mountains to appreciate their greatness. Men close about us make impression of their faults as well as excellencies. When men are at a distance we lose the sense of friction; we are not vexed by their eccentricities; and their merits rise conspicuous above all their limitations and imperfections of character. The heroism of yesterday seems always of a little finer quality than any courage we can find about us in the living men and women of to-day. The good of our generation are not quite so good as the good of the generations gone by. It does not seem to us there · is so much love, so much purity, so much devotion, so much energy of faith, so much perception of right and so much uncompromising fidelity to duty in the moral equipment of the world as there used to be. So it comes about that at any given time there is more or less of lamentation over the decline of piety. It is so now.

To hear some men talk, one would infer that there is very little personal attachment to Jesus and that what little there is, is growing all the while less. It is forgotten that what we read in the New Testament is largely the standard and not the record of attainment in the Christian life, and that so much of what is written is in the form of counsel and exhortation and rebuke. Judged by any fair rule, my candid conviction is that there never has been a time since our Divine Lord hung on the cross at Calvary when so many hearts were held to Him by the bond of a love so deep and sincere and abiding, when He was so much to such large numbers and classes as at the present hour. It is only a blind pessimism in which a Christian has no right to share that judges otherwise.

In confirmation of this opinion let me quote words spoken by Ex-President Porter a few years since in a baccalaureate sermon. "The new life," he says, "and the new rules of life have steadily gained upon the old. Christendom is far enough from being thoroughly Christlike or Christian in its living and thinking; but there never was a time when the

aims and the tastes, the loves and the hates, the principles and the maxims of the human race were more
Christianized than they are at the present moment.
Christian thought and Christian feeling, Christian
motives and Christian self-sacrifice, Christian purity
and refinement, Christian manners and tastes, Christian philosophy and jurisprudence and literature
were never more distinctly recognized and fervently
loved than at this moment."

These are the declarations of a man competent to
judge; and they are true. Put any generation, any
century of the past, side by side with this generation
or this century, and the facts will be found to warrant the conclusion. Large numbers are devoted to
Christ because they love Him and delight in His
service.

It is indeed one of the most cheering signs of the
times that no truth interests us like Christ. Christ
and the great doctrine of salvation and life through
Christ have an unmistakable power over souls. Devout spirits in all the church of God manifest an unwonted eagerness, through the clearest forms and the
sweetest, freshest imagery, to be brought face to face
with the God-Man, and made to feel that they are in
the breathing presence and under the hallowed spell
of the incarnate Son. We are told often that this
age which is pleased to call itself advanced,
cultivated and all that, can be expected to
have an interest only in things poetic or æsthetic
or scientific. It is true men are attracted by

fine thought, finely articulated. But nothing takes hold on the heart like the simple story of Him who suffered for us. Whoever can tell the *Old, Old Story* freshly, whether in pulpit or on platform or out in the open air or through the printed page, and put the facts of the life of our Lord into new form, and throw new light upon what He said and did; whoever can give us a new sense of the warm and sweet and measureless love He feels for men, — may be sure of responses which will testify to the affectionate regard and reverent loyalty in which He is held. Mr. Moody's wonderful success lies chiefly in the resolute fidelity with which he holds forth Christ. The one thing which will live beyond any peradventure in Dr. Bushnell's *Nature and Supernatural* is his incomparable chapter on Christ. The readiness with which the market absorbs so many lives of Christ, like Farrar's and Edersheim's, has its explanation in part in the eager interest with which Christian men and women follow the career and dwell on every detail which enters into the record of Jesus. Faces which shine because they have been close to the face of Jesus in the mount are everywhere about us. Much as there is to pain and discourage, the hearts of His people are very near the heart of their Lord. The breathings and hungerings of the church are toward Christ. In life and death, in struggles and sorrows, men cling to Jesus.

It is a touching picture, illustrative and typical of

what is taking place with increasing frequency in the earth, which Hare has given us of the closing hours of Baron Bunsen. "Many," he said, "had endeavored to build all kinds of bridges to eternal happiness; but he had come to the full conviction that all these bridges must be broken down; . . . as there was nothing to hold fast by except the simple faith in Christ." "It is sweet to die," he added. "With all feebleness and imperfection I have ever lived, and striven after and willed the best and noblest only. But the best and highest is to have known Jesus Christ."

2. Looking outward instead of inward, we find the influence of Jesus to be potent upon action. He molds character and conduct. The best things going on in the world may be cited in evidence.

There have been eras in the church which were predominantly meditative. Men loved Jesus; but they showed their love not in holy activities, but by withdrawing into cloisters where they could reflect on Him in an undisturbed seclusion. These men, not a few of them, rendered an enduring service to mankind; and the lovers of devout literature will not fail to acknowledge indebtedness to them.

Ours is not such an age. Whatever may be charged against the present, it can not truthfully be said that its faith is without works. The church as well as the world is alive with energy. Jesus said: "If ye love me, keep my commandments." Men are heeding the commandments, and under the influence of the teaching of Jesus and of His example they are doing such things and in such a large, wise way as can not be matched in all history. Hands of helpfulness are stretched out in a manner and to an extent wholly without precedent.

Take, for instance, the general benevolence of our modern days. There is an established habit of giving. The opulent, either while living or at death, are expected to share some portion of their wealth with the public. The old parsimony of the drama is no longer common. There has come to be a tacit admission on the part of Crœsus that he holds his gold in trust for his fellow-creatures. It is a fashion to be generous with money. The coming historian who shall look back and describe our days will be forced by his materials to recognize the liberality and the charity of the age. For the practice of giving and of giving with reference to the accomplishment of some good and wise end is well-nigh universal. It sweeps up from the widow to the millionaire.

It is because the spirit and example of Jesus Christ are making themselves felt more and more in the common heart of humanity. The law of His love has touched men inwardly, and their hands open and their purses open. Not all who give and give generously and wisely, are pronounced followers of our Lord; but they have felt His quickening breath, and they have been leavened, though all unconsciously, by His heavenly disposition.

The world we live in is still a sad one; and the cry of the human pierces the ear at every turn; and the mean men are many and the niggards are many and the heartless men whose one law of life is to get but never to give are many; but never before was the earth so bright with love, and never before were there so many tokens to be discovered of the tender regard which man feels for man, as in this nineteenth century.

Indeed, with schools for all classes and colors and conditions constantly springing up; with hospitals taking their places in all well-regulated communities as established institutions; with asylums opening their doors to the orphaned; with foundling homes, telling their woful tale, it is true, of sin and misery, but also of a sweet, beneficent care; with special provisions made so bountifully for the deaf and dumb and blind and insane; with organization after organization coming into existence, not only to check crime in its beginnings but to encourage self-help; with such a universal willingness to care for the poor and the reckless and the condemned even, and to minister up to the full measure of ability and requirement, to the unfortunate of every sort; with churches and Sunday-schools and societies of various kinds for the propagation of Christian truth and the exerting of Christian influence multiplying as never before, all up and down the land; and with missionaries of the cross in augmenting numbers pressing their way to the ends of the earth, — is it not patent that Jesus is an increasing moral force in society; and that men and communities of men are coming all the time more and more under the constraining might of His great, divine love?

If to this list of beneficent activities there be added the new sense of justice to which the nations are awaking in virtue of the influence of the lessons taught by Jesus, and the clearer expression and the deeper entrenchment which it is felt righteousness ought to have in human laws and institutions, as seen in the efforts to accord woman a higher place in the general economy of life, and to reconcile capital and labor by securing a more equitable distribution of the joint products of money and muscle, and the determined and prodigious endeavor which is one of the marked signs of the times to rid the world of what is at once the vice and the crime and the measureless curse of intemperance,— it will be seen that nothing is lacking in the way of proof or of illustration that the movement of Jesus is forward, and that as the years multiply His power advances.

Now observe the contrast between what Christ was when John discoursed concerning Him and what He is to-day, and it will appear with what unflagging energy the simple words which fell from the Baptist's lips have been sweeping on to their fulfillment.

Then human reason and conviction were against Him. Then the power of the earth was against Him. Then the hearts of men were against Him. A little company was ready to confess Him divine. A few feeble followers who were to forsake Him and flee away in His hour of need, made up the sole earthly force under His control. A small band, hardly any of whom understood Him fully, and some of whom ever followed Him afar off, were all who gave Him their affections. The *Head*, the *Hand* and the *Heart* of the world stood in triple array against Him. To-day it is not too much to affirm that the highest scholarship and the best learning are Christian. To-day the foremost nations on the globe are Christian. To-day Jesus is loved by millions and millions of hearts as is no other.

Still the word is: "*He must increase.*" So He will till His glory fills the earth and lights up the heavens with a splendor which shall outshine the brightness of the sun. — *Amen and Amen.*

THE END.